AAT

Spreadsheets for Accounting

Level 3
Advanced Diploma in Accounting
Course Book

For assessments to June 2023

Fifth edition 2021

ISBN 9781 5097 4212 7
ISBN (for internal use only) 9781 5097 4211 0

British Library Cataloguing-in-Publication Data
A catalogue record for this book is available from the
British Library

Published by

BPP Learning Media Ltd
BPP House, Aldine Place
142-144 Uxbridge Road
London W12 8AA

www.bpp.com/learningmedia

Printed in the United Kingdom

BPP
LEARNING MEDIA

Contents

Introduction to the course

Syllabus overview

This unit is about using spreadsheets to accurately enter, analyse and present information so that informed accountancy judgements can be made. The skills and knowledge from this unit integrates spreadsheet use within the other Level 3 subjects.

Accounting technicians need to use spreadsheets as it is important that financial information is accurately analysed and presented in an unambiguous way. Spreadsheets are widely used within industry, commerce and practice, and a variety of spreadsheet packages are available to assist with accounting roles including calculations, manipulation of data, analysis, budgeting, preparing financial statements, reporting, forecasting and decision making.

Students will add value to their organisation if they are familiar with the underlying principles of such software and can use it within their workplace. Completing this unit will allow students to apply these important skills to Advanced Bookkeeping, Final Accounts Preparation, Management Accounting: Costing and Indirect Tax.

Students will be able to analyse data using their spreadsheet skills and then communicate the most important information to enable appropriate judgements to be made. This means the information presented needs to be accurate and easily understood by the recipient.

The objective of this unit is to equip students with sufficient skills and knowledge to enable them to select the appropriate information and accurately input raw data into a spreadsheet. Students may have to use spreadsheets developed by others, or can produce their own. Students will need to demonstrate a range of skills to analyse data in line with accounting conventions. Skills such as the use of formulas, functions, data analysis tools including sorting and filtering will be vital when performing complex calculations quickly and accurately. After analysis, the data needs to be comprehensively checked and presented using a range of methods; for example, structured spreadsheets with pivot tables and charts. The responsibility for checking accuracy of information at Level 3 remains with the student.

Assessment method	Marking type	Duration of assessment
Assignment	Human marked	1 hour 30 minutes

Learning outcomes for Spreadsheets for Accounting		Weighting
1	Design and structure appropriate spreadsheets to meet customer needs	10%
2	Use spreadsheet software to record, format and organise data	30%
3	Use relevant tools to manipulate and analyse data	30%
4	Use software tools to verify accuracy and protect data	15%
5	Use tools and techniques to prepare and report accounting information	15%
		100%

Assessment structure

Students will be able to download the assignment brief and workbook securely through AAT's assessment platform. Students will have seven days to submit their completed assessment and other evidence.

The assessment workbook can be completed by students at the training provider / assessment venue but can also be completed without supervision.

The assessment is designed to be completed in 1 hour and 30 minutes. Students should not take any longer than 2 hours to complete all the tasks.

Students are required to complete a declaration of authenticity before the completed workbook is submitted. This declaration must also be completed and countersigned by the assessment centre, then submitted with the workbook.

Note that this is only a guideline as to what might come up. The format and content of each task may vary from what we have listed below.

The assessment will consist of 5 tasks with a total of 35 marks. This information is correct as at June 2021, however you are advised to check the AAT website for any changes that may have been introduced.

Assessment grading

The Spreadsheet for Accounting assessment is the only assessment in the Level 3 qualification that will not contribute towards the overall qualification grade. The assessment will be graded as pass / unclassified only. As with the other Level 3 subjects, a pass is 70%. Students must successfully achieve the assessment in order to gain the qualification.

Practice assessments

A practice Spreadsheet for Accounting assessment is available on the AAT website.

Do I need access to Excel software to use this Course Book?

Students must have access to a suitable spreadsheet software package as part of their studies for this unit and for the assessment. The assessment must be submitted in .xlsx format.

Students who do not have Excel software may still pick up some useful information from this Course Book. However, those students with access to Excel will find it easier to work through the practical exercises than users of other spreadsheet software packages.

Why does this Course Book refer to Excel 2010 and Excel 2013?

To explain and demonstrate the skills required in this unit, it is necessary to provide practical examples and exercises. This requires the use of spreadsheet software. This Course Book provides examples taken from Excel 2010 and Excel 2013.

Microsoft releases new versions of its software every few years, each time hoping to offer technical and user improvements. The basic functions are often the same.

Students should study **either** Chapters 1 and 2 (covering Excel 2010) **or** Chapters 3 and 4 (covering Excel 2013).

What version of Excel do I need?

The illustrations in this book are taken from Excel 2010 and 2013.

If you are using a different version of Excel you can still use this book. However, you may notice some differences in the way Excel operates in certain sections.

Are Excel data files available for use with this Course Book?

Yes. Excel data files are included, either to provide a starting set of data or to show the results of an exercise. You will be given instructions for locating the relevant spreadsheet when you need it.

The spreadsheets referred to in this Course Book are available for download – type https://learningmedia.bpp.com/catalog?pagename=AAT_Spreadsheets into your browser and follow the instructions provided.

Skills bank

Our experience of preparing students for this type of assessment suggests that to obtain competency, you will need to develop a number of key skills.

What do I need to know to do well in the Level 3 *Spreadsheets for Accounting* Assessment?

To be successful in the assessment you need to:

- Design and structure appropriate spreadsheets to meet customer needs
- Use spreadsheet software to record, format and organise data
- Use relevant tools to manipulate and analyse data
- Use software tools to verify accuracy and protect data
- Use tools and techniques to prepare and report accounting information

Assessment style

In the assessment you will complete tasks using **spreadsheet** software

You must familiarise yourself with the style of the questions and the spreadsheet software before taking the assessment. As part of your revision, login to the **AAT website** and attempt their **online practice assessments** within the **Lifelong Learning Portal**.

Spreadsheets for accounting				
⌄ E-learning				0/3 ●
⌃ Practice assessment	💬	👁		0/2 ●
Spreadsheets for accounting – practice assessment (assessable from September 2021)		⊘	●	0/1 ●
Spreadsheets for accounting – practice assessment workbook (assessable from September 2021)		⊘	●	0/1 ●

Introduction to the Level 3 *Spreadsheets for Accounting* Unit Assessment

The question practice you do will prepare you for the format of tasks you will see in the *Spreadsheets for Accounting* assessment. It is also useful to familiarise yourself with the introductory information you **may** be given at the start of the assessment. For example:

Assessment information

- You are required to open the Excel spreadsheet called 'Assessment workbook', which contains the data you require for this assessment.

- This assessment is closed book. You must not use any additional support material, other than the workbook provided to generate your evidence.

- You should read the task scenario and instructions carefully and complete all tasks. It should take you no longer than **2 hours** to complete all tasks.

- All work must be submitted for marking within 7 days of the assessment centre unlocking the assessment. Any work not uploaded within this time will **not** be marked.

- Before submitting your work for marking, you must sign the 'Declaration of authenticity' to confirm that you have not had help with this assessment. The declaration must also be completed and countersigned by your assessment centre, then submitted with your work. It is important that all work produced is your own. If you fail to confirm authenticity of work produced, your work will not be marked.

- If during the marking process we suspect impersonation, plagiarism, or any other form of malpractice an investigation will be carried out. Sanctions will be imposed, or disciplinary action taken if there is clear evidence that malpractice has taken place.

- Once your work has been submitted to AAT for marking, you must delete the task instructions and your assessment workbook from the PC and/or other equipment (eg USB) on which it has been stored. You must not copy or share the task instructions or assessment workbook with anyone else.

Information

- The paper is designed to be completed within 1 hour 30 minutes and should not take you longer than 2 hours.

- This assessment has a total of **5 tasks** which are divided into subtasks.

- The total mark for this paper is 35.

- The data you need to complete a task is contained within that task or through the pop-up that appears on the task page; you will not need to refer to your answers for previous tasks.

Advice

- Read each question carefully before you start to answer it.
- Attempt all questions.

This information is correct as at June 2021.

Key to icons

Key term	A key definition which is important to be aware of for the assessment
Formula to learn	A formula you will need to learn as it will not be provided in the assessment
Formula provided	A formula which is provided within the assessment and generally available as a pop-up on screen
Activity	An example which allows you to apply your knowledge to the technique covered in the Course Book. The solution is provided at the end of the chapter
Illustration	A worked example which can be used to review and see how an assessment question could be answered
Assessment focus point	A high priority point for the assessment
Open book reference	Where use of an open book will be allowed for the assessment
Real life examples	A practical real life scenario

AAT qualifications

The material in this book may support the following AAT qualifications:

AAT Advanced Diploma in Accounting Level 3 and AAT Advanced Diploma in Accounting at SCQF Level 6.

Supplements

From time to time we may need to publish supplementary materials to one of our titles. This can be for a variety of reasons, from a small change in the AAT unit guidance to new legislation coming into effect between editions.

You should check our supplements page regularly for anything that may affect your learning materials. All supplements are available free of charge on our supplements page on our website at:

https://learningmedia.bpp.com/catalog?pagename=Errata

Online information specific to this course book

Due to the nature of the course which requires the practice and understanding of using spreadsheets, we have provided additional online resources which may be downloaded at the following location:

https://learningmedia.bpp.com/catalog?pagename=AAT_Spreadsheets

A zip file will allow you to download all the files you will need for this course. The files for the course book are kept in the folder AAT Spreadsheets

Improving material and removing errors

There is a constant need to update and enhance our study materials in line with both regulatory changes and new insights into the assessments.

From our team of authors BPP appoints a subject expert to update and improve these materials for each new edition.

Their updated draft is subsequently technically checked by another author and from time to time non-technically checked by a proof reader.

We are very keen to remove as many numerical errors and narrative typos as we can but given the volume of detailed information being changed in a short space of time we know that a few errors will sometimes get through our net.

We apologise in advance for any inconvenience that an error might cause. We continue to look for new ways to improve these study materials and would welcome your suggestions. Please feel free to contact our AAT Head of Programme at nisarahmed@bpp.com if you have any suggestions for us.

These learning materials are based on the qualification specification released by the AAT in April 2021.

Introduction to spreadsheets (Excel 2010)

1

Learning outcomes

1.1	**Organise data in a timely manner**
	Students need to be able to:
	- Identify all customer requirements, including deadlines
	- Consider the use of a template or design a bespoke spreadsheet
	- Plan and design the spreadsheet to meet customer needs
	- Develop a spreadsheet for specific accountancy purposes
2.1	**Select relevant data**
	Students need to know:
	- When they have sufficient data and information
	Students need to be able to:
	- Select valid, reliable and accurate data
	- Select relevant raw data from different sources
	- Differentiate between what information is required and what information is not required
2.3	**Format data**
	Students need to be able to:
	- Use a range of appropriate formatting tools to aid understanding and present the data effectively
3.1	**Select and use a range of appropriate formulas and functions to perform calculations**
	Students need to be able to:
	- Plan, select and use a range of formulas to manipulate and analyse the data
	- Plan, select and use appropriate mathematical and logical functions and statistical techniques to perform calculations

3.3	**Select and use appropriate tools to generate and format charts**
	Students need to be able to:
	• Critically select and use a range of charts to summarise and present information
	• Develop and format charts appropriately to aid understanding
	– Altering scales
	– Altering formatting axes
	– Labelling charts
	– Change data series colour and/or format
	• Produce an output in a format suitable to ensure equality of opportunity
5.1	**Prepare reports**
	Students need to be able to:
	• Insert headers and footers
	• Hide rows and/or columns
	• Format columns, rows and outputs to enhance understanding of the relevant data
	• Adjust margins, orientation and print area
	• Produce a summary sheet linking to other data and/or worksheets
5.2	**Report accounting information**
	Students need to know:
	• Why it is important to confirm that the result meets customer requirements
	Students need to be able to:
	• Ensure that data produced is suitable for publication, using the appropriate house style
	• Show all worksheet formulas in a format suitable for publication
	• Communicate the completed information to the customer appropriately

Assessment context

The *Spreadsheets for Accounting* unit is assessed as part of the Level 3 *Advanced Diploma in Accounting* Unit Assessment. You will be requested to present your answers in an appropriate spreadsheet format to show a whole range of skills and knowledge.

Qualification context

Specific spreadsheet software use only appears on the *Spreadsheets for Accounting* unit; however, some of the concepts used, for example saving files, use of passwords and accurate input of data may be familiar to you either from use of spreadsheets or from experience using other software packages.

Business context

The use of spreadsheet packages are a vital part of business life. Spreadsheets are known for their speed and accuracy in calculations and also their data manipulation capabilities. This means that spreadsheets are indispensable in the work of accountants and other finance professionals.

Chapter overview

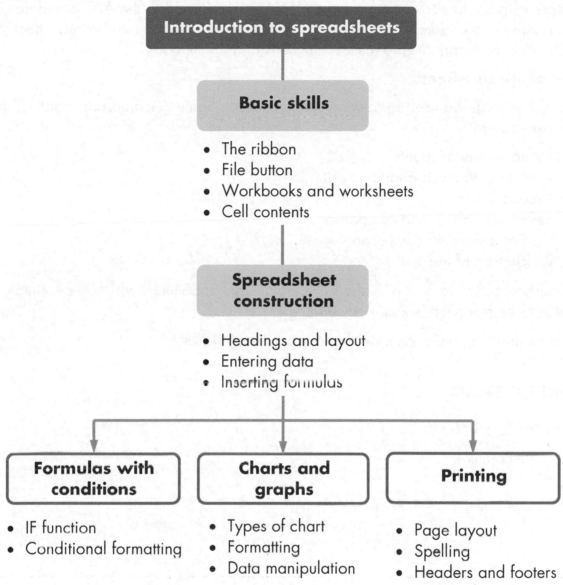

Introduction to spreadsheets

Basic skills

- The ribbon
- File button
- Workbooks and worksheets
- Cell contents

Spreadsheet construction

- Headings and layout
- Entering data
- Inserting formulas

Formulas with conditions

- IF function
- Conditional formatting

Charts and graphs

- Types of chart
- Formatting
- Data manipulation

Printing

- Page layout
- Spelling
- Headers and footers
- Printing formulas
- Annotating output

Introduction

The vast majority of people who work in an accounting environment are required to use spreadsheets to perform their duties. This fact is reflected in the AAT Standards, which require candidates to be able to produce clear, well-presented spreadsheets, which utilise appropriate spreadsheet functions and formulas.

Uses of spreadsheets

Spreadsheets can be used for a wide range of tasks. Some common applications of spreadsheets are:

- Management accounts
- Cash flow analysis and forecasting
- Reconciliations
- Revenue analysis and comparison
- Cost analysis and comparison
- Budgets and forecasts

Spreadsheet software also provides basic database capabilities, which allow simple records to be recorded, sorted and searched.

In this section we revise some **basic spreadsheet skills**.

1 Basic skills

1.1 The Ribbon

1.2 File button

The **File** button is a menu button and provides access to several options.

1.3 Workbooks and worksheets

At the bottom left of the spreadsheet window you will see tabs which are known as **Worksheets**:

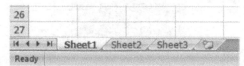

When **New** is selected from the Office button menu, a new **workbook** is created. The workbook consists of one or more **worksheets**. Think of worksheets as **pages** that make up the workbook. By default, a new Excel workbook starts out with three worksheets, although this can be changed (see later).

Worksheets can provide a convenient way of organising information. For example, consider a business consisting of three branches. Worksheets 2–4 could hold budget information separately for each branch. When entering formulas into cells it is possible to refer to cells in other worksheets within the workbook, so it would then be possible for Worksheet 1 to act as a **summary sheet** linking the totals of the budget information for the whole business. Effectively, a 'three-dimensional' structure can be set up. We look at this in more detail later.

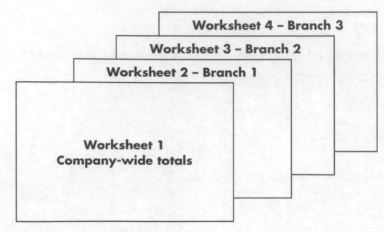

Worksheet 4 – Branch 3

Worksheet 3 – Branch 2

Worksheet 2 – Branch 1

**Worksheet 1
Company-wide totals**

Opening an existing workbook

You can open an existing workbook file by using the menu commands **File button>Open** and then navigating to the location of the file and double-clicking on it.

If you open more than one workbook, each will open in a new window. To swap between open workbooks, click on the **File button** and choose the workbook you want from the **Recent documents** list.

Closing a workbook

There are two ways to close a spreadsheet file:

(1) Click the **File button** and choose **Close** (fourth icon down)

(2) Click on either the '**x**' in the top right-hand corner of the window or the one just below it.

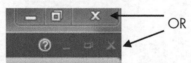

OR

In both cases, if you have made any changes to the spreadsheet you will be asked if you want to save them. Choose **Yes** to save any changes (this will overwrite the existing file), **No** to close the file without saving any changes, or **Cancel** to return to the spreadsheet.

1.4 Cell contents

The contents of any cell can be one of the following:

(a) **Text**. A text cell usually contains **words**. Numbers that do not represent numeric values for calculation purposes (eg a Part Number) may be entered in a way that tells Excel to treat the cell contents as text. To do this, enter an apostrophe before the number: '451, for example.

(b) **Values**. A value is a **number** that can be used in a calculation.

(c) **Formulas**. A formula **refers to other cells** in the spreadsheet, and performs some type of computation with them. For example, if cell C1 contains the formula =A1 – B1, cell C1 will display the result of the calculation, subtracting the contents of cell B1 from the contents of cell A1. In Excel, a formula always begins with an equals sign: = . This alerts the program that what follows is a formula and not text or a value. There is a wide range of formulas and functions available.

Illustration 1: Cell contents

Open the workbook called 'ExcelExample1'. This is one of the files available for download from https://learningmedia.bpp.com/catalog?pagename =AAT_Spreadsheets. You can open a file by using the menu commands:

File button>Open

then navigating to, and double-clicking on, the file called 'ExcelExample1'.

Note. Throughout this Course Book we want spreadsheets to recalculate every time a figure is changed. This is the normal or default setting, so it is likely your spreadsheets already do this. But, if they don't, then:

(1) Click the **File Button**, click **Excel Options**, and then click the **Formulas** category.

(2) To recalculate all dependent formulas every time you make a change to a value, formula or name, in the **Calculation options** section, under **Workbook Calculation**, click **Automatic**. This is the default calculation setting.

	A	B	C	D	E
1	BUDGETED SALES FIGURES				
2		Jan	Feb	Mar	Total
3		£'000	£'000	£'000	£'000
4	North	2,431	3,001	2,189	7,621
5	South	6,532	5,826	6,124	18,482
6	West	895	432	596	1,923
7	Total	9,858	9,259	8,909	28,026
8					

E4 f_x =B4+C4+D4 ← Formula shown in formula bar

When you open ExcelExample1 you should see the worksheet illustrated above.

Click on cell E4.

Look at the formula bar.

Note. If the formula bar is not visible, choose the **View** tab and check the **Formula Bar** box.

Note the important difference between:

(1) What is shown in cell E4: 7,621.

(2) What is actually in cell E4: this is shown in the formula bar and it tells us that cell E4 is the result of adding together the contents of cells B4, C4 and D4.

The formula bar allows you to see and edit the contents of the active cell. The bar also shows, on the left side, the cell address of the active cell (E4 in the illustration above).

Select different cells to be the active cell by using the up/down/right/left arrows on your keyboard or by clicking directly on the cell you want to be active. Look at what is in the cell and what is shown in the formula bar.

The **F5** key is useful for moving around within large spreadsheets. If you press the function key **F5**, a **Go To** dialogue box will allow you to specify the cell address you would like to move to. Try this out.

Also experiment by holding down **Ctrl** and pressing each of the direction arrow keys in turn to see where you end up. Try using the **Page Up** and **Page Down** keys and also try **Home** or **End**, and **Ctrl** with these keys. Try **Tab** or **Shift** /**Tab**, too. These are all useful shortcuts for moving quickly from one place to another in a large spreadsheet.

When dealing with large worksheets it can be useful to **Freeze** rows or columns so that specified ranges of data (eg headings) remain 'frozen' while scrolling and navigating throughout a worksheet. To do this select the data you wish frozen and select your choice by going to **View>Freeze Panes**.

Examples of spreadsheet formulas

Formulas in Microsoft Excel follow a specific syntax. All Excel formulas start with the equals sign =, followed by the elements to be calculated (the operands) and the calculation operators (such as +, –, /, *). Each operand can be a:

- Value that does not change (a constant value, such as the VAT rate)

- Cell or range reference to a range of cells

- Name (a named cell, such as 'VAT')

- Worksheet function (such as 'AVERAGE', which will work out the average value of defined values)

Formulas can be used to perform a variety of calculations. Here are some examples:

(a) =C4*5. This formula **multiplies** the value in C4 by 5. The result will appear in the cell holding the formula.

(b) =C4*B10. This **multiplies** the value in C4 by the value in B10.

(c) =C4/E5. This **divides** the value in C4 by the value in E5. (* means multiply and / means divide by.)

(d)   =C4*B10–D1. This **multiplies** the value in C4 by that in B10 and then **subtracts** (or minus) the value in D1 from the result. Note that generally Excel will perform multiplication and division before addition or subtraction. If in any doubt, use brackets (parentheses): =(C4*B10)–D1.

(e)   =C4*120%. This **adds** 20% to the value in C4. It could be used to calculate a price including 20% VAT.

(f)   =(C4+C5+C6)/3. Note that the **brackets** mean Excel would perform the addition first. Without the brackets, Excel would first divide the value in C6 by 3 and then add the result to the total of the values in C4 and C5.

(g)   = 2^2 gives you 2 **to the power** of 2, in other words 2 squared. Likewise = 2^3 gives you 2 cubed and so on.

(h)   = 4^(1/2) gives you the **square root** of 4. Likewise 27^(1/3) gives you the cube root of 27 and so on.

Displaying spreadsheet formulas

It is sometimes useful to see all formulas held in your spreadsheet to enable you to see how the spreadsheet works. There are two ways of making Excel **display the formulas** held in a spreadsheet.

(a)   You can 'toggle' between the two types of display by pressing **Ctrl** +` (the latter is the key above the **Tab** key). Press **Ctrl** +` again to go back to the previous display.

(b)   You can also click on **Formulas>Show Formulas** in the Ribbon.

The formulas for the spreadsheet we viewed earlier are shown below.

	A	B	C	D	E
1	BUDGETED S				
2		Jan	Feb	Mar	Total
3		£'000	£'000	£'000	£'000
4	North	2431	3001	2189	=B4+C4+D4
5	South	6532	5826	6124	=B5+C5+D5
6	West	895	432	596	=B6+C6+D6
7	Total	=B4+B5+B6	=C4+C5+C6	=D4+D5+D6	=E4+E5+E6

The importance of formulas

Look carefully at the example above and note which cells have formulas in them. It is important to realise that:

- If a cell contains a value, such as sales for North in January, then that data is entered as a number

- If a cell shows the result of a calculation based on values in other cells, such as the total sales for January, then that cell contains a formula

This is vital, because now if North's January sales were changed to, say, 2,500, the total would be automatically updated to show 9,927. Also the total for North would change to 7,690.

Try that out by clicking on cell B4 to make it active, then typing 2,500, followed by the **Enter** key. You should see both the totals change.

Now re-enter the original figure of 2,431 into cell B4.

Similarly, if a number is used more than once, for example a tax rate, it will be much better if the number is input to one cell only. Any other calculations making use of that value should refer to that cell. That way, if the tax rate changes, you only have to change it in one place in the spreadsheet (where it was originally entered) and any calculations making use of it will automatically change.

Your first function

In the example above, totals were calculated using a formula such as:

=+B4+C4+D4

That is fine, provided there are not too many items to be included in the total. Imagine the difficulty if you had to find the total of 52 weeks for a year. Adding up rows or columns is made much easier by using the **SUM** function. Instead of the formula above, we could place the following calculation in cell E4:

= SUM(B4:D4)

This produces the sum of all the cells in the range B4 to D4. Now it is much easier to add up a very long row of figures (for example, SUM(F5:T5)) or a very long column of figures (for example, SUM(B10:B60)).

There are three ways in which the SUM function can be entered. One way is simply to type =SUM(B4:D4) when E4 is the active cell. However, there is a more visual and, perhaps, more accurate way.

Make E4 the active cell by moving the cursor to it using the arrow keys or by clicking on it.

Type =**Sum(**
Click on cell B4
Type a colon **:**
Click on cell D4
Close the bracket by typing **)**
Press the **Enter** key

Editing cell contents

Cell D5 of ExcelExample1 currently contains the value 6,124. If you wish to change the value in that cell from 6,124 to 6,154 there are four options (you have already used the first method).

(a) Activate cell D5, type 6,154 and press **Enter**.

To undo this and try the next option press **Ctrl + Z**; this will always undo what you have just done (a very useful shortcut).

(b) **Double-click** in cell D5. The cell will keep its thick outline but you will now be able to see a vertical line flashing in the cell. You can move this line by using the direction arrow keys or the **Home** and the **End** keys. Move it to just after the 2, press the **backspace** key on the keyboard and then type 5. Then press **Enter**. (Alternatively, move the vertical line to just in front of the 2, press the **Delete** key on the keyboard, then type 5, followed by the **Enter** key).

When you have tried this press **Ctrl + Z** to undo it.

(c) **Click once** before the number 6,124 in the formula bar. Again, you will get the vertical line which can be moved back and forth to allow editing as in (b) above.

(d) Activate cell D4 and press **F2** at the top of your keyboard. The vertical line cursor will be flashing in cell D4 at the end of the figures entered there and this can be used to edit the cell contents, as above.

Deleting cell contents

There are a number of ways to delete the contents of a cell:

(a) Make the cell the active cell and press the **Delete** button. The contents of the cell will disappear.

(b) Go to the **Editing** section on the **Home** tab of the Ribbon. Click on the **Clear** button and various options appear. Click **Clear Contents**. You can also achieve this by **right-clicking** the cell and choosing **Clear Contents**.

Any **cell formatting** (for example, cell colour or border) will not be removed when using either of these methods. To remove formatting click on the **Clear** button on the **Home** tab and select **Clear Formats**. If you want to remove the formatting and the contents, click **Clear All**.

Ranges of cells

A range of cells can occupy a single column or row or can be a rectangle of cells. The extent of a range is defined by the rectangle's top-left cell reference and the bottom-right cell reference. If the range is within a single row or column, it is defined by the references of the start and end cells.

Defining a range is very useful, as you can then manipulate many cells at once rather than having to go to each one individually.

The following shows that a rectangular range of cells has been selected from C4 to D6. The range consists of three rows and two columns.

	A	B	C	D	E	F
1	BUDGETED SALES FIGURES					
2		Jan	Feb	Mar	Total	
3		£'000	£'000	£'000	£'000	
4	North	2,431	3,001	2,189	7,621	
5	South	6,532	5,826	6,124	18,482	
6	West	895	432	596	1,923	
7	Total	9,858	9,259	8,909	28,026	
8						
9						

There are several ways of selecting ranges. Try the following:

(1) Click on cell C4, but hold the mouse button down. Drag the cursor down and to the right until the required range has been selected. Then release the mouse button. Now press the **Delete** key. All the cells in this range are cleared of their contents. Reverse this by **Ctrl+Z** and deselect the range by clicking on any single cell.

(2) Click on cell C4 (release the mouse button). Hold down the **Shift** key and press the **down** and **right-hand arrows** on your keyboard until the correct range is highlighted.

Deselect the range by clicking on any single cell.

(3) Click on cell C4 (release the mouse button). Hold down the **Shift** key and click on cell D6.

Deselect the range by clicking on any single cell.

(4) Sometimes you may want to select an entire row or column:

Say you wanted to select row 3, perhaps to change all the occurrences of £'000 to a bold font. Position your cursor over the figure 3 defining row 3 and click. All of row 3 is selected. Clicking on the **B** in the font group on the **Home** tab will make the entire row bold:

Whole spread-sheet selection

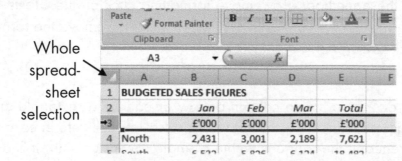

(5) Sometimes you may want to select every cell in the worksheet, perhaps to put everything into a different font:

Click on the triangle shape at the extreme top-left of the cells (indicated above). Alternatively you can select the active cells using **Ctrl + A**.

There are a number of labour-saving shortcuts which allow you to quickly fill ranges of cells with headings (such as £'000, or month names) and with patterns of numbers. You can keep the 'ExcelExercise1' spreadsheet open throughout the following activities and simply open a new spreadsheet on which to experiment.

Illustration 2: Using the fill handle

(1) Create a new spreadsheet **(File button>New.** Select **Blank workbook.)**

(2) Make cell B3 active and type Jan (or January) into it.

(3) Position the cursor at the bottom right of cell B3 (you will see a black **+** when you are at the right spot – this is often referred to as the **fill handle**).

(4) Hold down the mouse button and drag the cursor rightwards, until it is under row G. Release the mouse button.

The month names will automatically fill across.

(5) Using the same technique, fill B4 to G4 with £.

(6) Type 'Region' into cell 3A.

(7) Type the figure 1 into cell A5 and 2 into cell A6. Select the range A5–A6 and obtain the black cross **+** at the bottom right of cell A6. Hold down the mouse key and drag the cursor down to row 10. Release the mouse button.

The figures 1–6 will automatically fill down column A.

Note. If 1 and 3 had been entered into A5 and C6, then 1, 3, 5, 7, 9, 11 would automatically appear. This does **not** work if just the figure 1 is entered into A5.

Percentages

Percentages can be calculated using a formula, or by using the percentage function. When using a formula always remember to multiply your answer by 100. For example, to calculate 40 out of 200 as a percentage value the formula would be =(40/200)*100

Alternatively, the percentage function can be used instead. Using the same figures as above simply enter =40/200 and this will show a decimal value.

Then go to **Home**, **Number** and **Percentage**.

The decimal value will now be expressed as a percentage.

Copying and pasting formulas

You have already seen that formulas are extremely important in spreadsheet construction. In Excel it is very easy to define a formula once and then apply it to a wide range of cells. As it is applied to different cells the cell references in the formula are automatically updated. Say you wanted to multiply together each row of figures in columns A and B and to display the answer in the equivalent rows of column C.

Illustration 3: Copy and Paste

(1) Make C1 the active cell.

(2) Type **=**, then click on cell A1, then type * and click on cell B1.

(3) Press **Enter**.

The formula =A1*B1 should be shown in the formula bar, and the amount 232,800 should be shown in C1.

(4) Make C1 the active cell and obtain the black **+** by positioning the cursor at the bottom right of that cell.

(5) Hold down the mouse button and drag the cursor down to row 5.

(6) Release the mouse button.

Look at the formulas in column C. You will see that the cell references change as you move down the column, updating as you move from row to row.

C3		f_x	=A3*B3	
	A	B	C	D
1	400	582	232800	
2	250	478	119500	
3	359	264	94776	
4	476	16	7616	
5	97	125	12125	

It is also possible to copy whole blocks of cells, with formulas being updated in a logical way.

(1) Make A1 the active cell and select the range A1:C5, for example, by dragging the cursor down and rightwards.

(2) Press **Ctrl+C** (the standard Windows copy command) or click on the **Copy** symbol in the **Home** section of the ribbon.

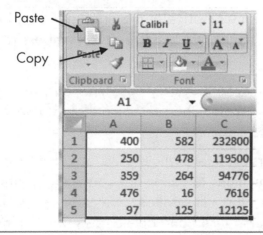

(3) Make E7 the active cell and press **Ctrl+V** or click on the **paste** button. E7 will become the top-right cell of the copied rectangle and will hold 400.

(4) Now, look at the formula shown in cell G7. It will show =E7*F7. So all cell references in the formulas have been updated relative to one another. This type of copying is called **relative copying**.

(5) **Delete** the range E7:G7.

Sometimes you don't want to copy a formula and you only want to copy the displayed values. This can be done using **Paste special**.

Illustration 4: Paste special

Open the spreadsheet called 'Paste special example' from the files available for download at
https://learningmedia.bpp.com/catalog?pagename=AAT_Spreadsheets.

You will see a simple inventory-type application listing quantities, prices and values. The values are obtained by formulas multiplying together prices and quantities. Say that you just want to copy the values of cells D3:D8, without the underlying formulas.

(1) Select the range D3:D8.

(2) Press **Ctrl+C** or the copy icon in the **Clipboard** part of **Home** on the Ribbon.

(3) **Right-click** on cell C12 to make it active, and choose **Paste Special** from the list.

(4) Check the **Values** radio button.

(5) Click **OK**.

The list of figures will be pasted, but if you look in the formula bar, you will see that they are just figures; there are no formulas there.

Note. If you change a quantity or price in the original table, the figures you have just pasted will not change; they have become pure numbers and do not link back to their source.

Cells can be linked between worksheets by copying and pasting links. This can be achieved by selecting, and copying the cell value that you wish to link, then go to **Home>Paste>Paste Link**.

Often you will need to insert or delete whole rows or columns in spreadsheets. This can easily be done and sometimes formulas are correctly updated – but they should always be checked. For this illustration we will go back to using the 'ExcelExample1' spreadsheet to insert and delete rows or columns

Illustration 5: Using insert and delete

Close the spreadsheet you have recently been working on and go back to (using the tabs across the bottom of the screen), or reopen, the spreadsheet 'ExcelExample1'.

Let us assume that we have a new region, East, and that we want this to be in a row lying between North and South.

(1) Select row 5, by clicking on the 5, then click the right mouse button (right-click) and select **Insert**. You will see rows 5, 6 and 7 move down.

(2) Make B8 the active cell and you will see that the formula in the formula bar is =B4+B6+B7. If we were to put the figures for East into row 5 then those would **not** be correctly included in the total, though B5 has been updated to B6 etc.

(3) Reverse the last step (**Ctrl+Z**).

(4) Now, in cell B7 insert =SUM(B4:B6).

(5) Copy B7 across columns C7 to E7 (black cross and drag across).

(6) Check the formulas that are in cells C7 to E7 to ensure they have all been updated.

(7) Insert a whole row above row 5 (select row 5>right-click>**Insert**).

(8) Inspect the formulas in row 8, the new total row.

The formulas in the total row will now be showing =SUM(B4:B7), =SUM(C4:C7), etc. In this case the new row will be included in the total. Effectively, the range over which the totals are calculated has been 'stretched'. Depending how your copy of Excel is set up, you may notice little green triangles in row 8. If so, place your cursor on one and press the exclamation symbol. The triangles are warning that you have included empty cells in your total – not a problem here, but it might have been in some cases. Don't worry if the triangles aren't showing.

(9) Finally, delete row 5. Select the whole row by clicking on the 5, then right-click and choose **Delete** from the menu.

The cells below Row 5 will move up and the SUM formulas are again updated.

New columns can also be added. Say that we now wanted to include April in the results.

(1) Replace the current formula in E4 with =SUM(B4:D4).

(2) Copy the formula in E4 down through columns 5, 6 and 7. Check that the correct formulas are in cells E4–E7.

(3) Select column E, by clicking on the E, then click the right mouse button (right-click) and select **Insert**. You will see column E move to the right.

(4) Inspect the formulas now in Column F, the new total column.

You will see that the formula in F7 still says = SUM(B7:D7). It has **not been updated** for the extra column.

So, if an extra row or column is inserted in the middle of a range, the formulas is updated because the new row or column probably (but not always) becomes part of the range that has to be added up.

However, if the extra row or column is added at the end of a range (or the start) the formula will not be updated to include that. That's reasonably logical as new items at the very start or end have a greater chance of being headings or something not part of the range to be included in a calculation.

Assessment focus point

Whenever columns or rows are added or deleted always check that formulas affected remain correct.

Changing column width and row height

You may occasionally find that a cell is not wide enough to display its contents. When this occurs, the cell displays a series of hashes ######. There are several ways to deal with this problem:

- Column widths can be adjusted by positioning the mouse pointer at the head of the column, directly over the little line dividing two columns. The mouse **pointer** will change to a **cross** with a double-headed arrow through it. Hold down the left mouse button and, by moving your mouse, stretch or shrink the column until it is the right width. Alternatively, you can double-click when the double-headed arrow appears and the column will automatically adjust to the optimum width.

- Highlight the columns you want to adjust and choose **Home>Cells>Format>Column Width** from the menu and set the width manually. Alternatively, you can right-click the highlighted column(s) and choose **Column Width** from the menu.

- Highlight the columns you want to adjust and choose **Home>Format>AutoFit Column Width** from the menu and set the width to fit the contents.

Setting row heights works similarly.

Columns and rows can also be hidden from view by making the selection and going to **Home>Format>Hide & Unhide**.

Date and time stamps

Assessment focus point

Date and time stamps will not be an examined skill, however, we have left brief information here so you are aware how to use this in your working life.

You can insert the current date into a cell by **Ctrl+;** (semicolon)

You can insert the current time by **Ctrl+Shift+;**

You can insert date and time by first inserting the date, release **Ctrl**, press space, insert the time. The date can be formatted by going to **Home>Number>Date** and choosing the format required.

Once a date is entered it is easy to produce a sequence of dates.

Naming cells and ranges

Illustration 6: Naming cells and ranges

(1) Open the worksheet called 'Name example'.

(2) Make cell B3 the active one and right-click on it.

(3) Select **Name a range**.

(4) Accept the offered name, 'VAT', that Excel has picked up from the neighbouring cell.

(5) Highlight the range D4:D7, right-click **Name a range** and accept the offered 'Net'.

(6) In E4 enter =Net*(1 + VAT).

(7) Copy E4 into E5:E7.

You will see the formula bar refers to names. This makes understanding a spreadsheet much easier.

A list of names can be seen using the **Formulas** section of the Ribbon and clicking on **Name Manager**

Merging cells

Instead of entering text or values (numbers) into one column you may wish to enter your data so that it is merged across a number of columns. To do this go to **Home>Alignment** and select:

A merged cell looks like this: Merged cell

◢	A	B	C	D	E
1		Revenue			
2	Company	Jan	Feb	Mar	Apr
3	Annabel Limited	5000	5000	5000	5500
4	Beatrice & Co	12000	11500	13000	14000
5	Caroline Ltd	4000	3400	3500	4000
6	Delilah's Dressers	3000	4500	4000	4000
7					

Keyboard shortcuts

Here are a few tips to quickly improve the **appearance** of your spreadsheets and speed up your work, using only the keyboard. These are all alternatives to clicking the relevant button in the **Home** section of the Ribbon.

To do any of the following to a cell or range of cells, first **select** the cell or cells and then:

(a)   Press **Ctrl + B** to make the cell contents **bold**.

(b)   Press **Ctrl + I** to make the cell contents *italic.*

(c)   Press **Ctrl + U** to <u>underline</u> the cell contents.

(d)   Press **Ctrl + C** to **copy** the contents of the cells.

(e)   Move the cursor and press **Ctrl + V** to **paste** the cell you just copied into the new active cell or cells.

(f)   'Toggle' between the two types of display by pressing **Ctrl +`** (the latter is the key above the **Tab** key). Press **Ctrl +`** again to go back to the previous display.

2 Spreadsheet construction

All spreadsheets need to be planned and then constructed carefully. More complex spreadsheet models should include some documentation that explains how the spreadsheet is set up and how to use it. When constructing a spreadsheet it is important to select valid, relevant and reliable data and this can come from a variety of sources.

There can be a feeling that, because the spreadsheet carries out calculations automatically, results will be reliable. However, there can easily be errors in formulas, errors of principle and errors in assumptions. All too often, spreadsheets offer a reliable and quick way to produce nonsense.

Furthermore, it is rare for only one person to have to use or adapt a spreadsheet; proper documentation is important if other people are to be able to make efficient use of it. To assist with spreadsheet construction pre-designed templates can be used for purposes that may be common to multiple users. If a spreadsheet is of a specialist nature or is being constructed for a one-off purpose then the spreadsheet may be designed as bespoke or custom-made. Having the correct approach to spreadsheet construction can help ensure output meets user (or customer) requirements.

It is important to note that information has to be made available to users in a timely manner and communicated as appropriate. This is particularly important for financial information, where late delivery can result in penalties or other losses. This means that those who are responsible for spreadsheet construction need to observe any deadlines set, either by management or external agencies such as HM Revenue & Customs.

To help with communication and also branding, many organisations adopt a **house style** for their output. House style is a standardised set of rules for formatting to be used. Examples can include fonts, font size and text colour.

Assessment focus point

Look out for instructions on house style or formatting to be used on assessment tasks and always ensure that your formatting is consistent with the style requested.

The following should be kept in separate identifiable areas of the spreadsheet:

(1)   An inputs and assumptions section, containing the variables (eg the amount of a loan and the interest rate, planned mark-ups, assumptions about growth rates).

(2)   A calculations section containing formulas.

(3)   The results section, showing the outcome of the calculations.

Sometimes it is convenient to combine (2) and (3).

It is also important to consider the following:

(1)   Document data sources. For example, where did the assumed growth rate come from? If you don't know that, how will you ever test the validity of that data and any results arising from it?

(2)   Explain calculation methods. This is particularly important if calculations are complex or have to be done in a specified way.

(3)   Explain the variables used in functions. Some functions require several input variables (arguments) and may not be familiar to other users.

(4)   Set out the spreadsheet clearly, using underlinings, colour, bold text etc to assist users.

Illustration 7: Spreadsheet construction

Constructing a costing spreadsheet.

You want to set up a spreadsheet to record the time you and your colleagues spend on an assignment, and to cost it using your group's internal chargeout rates which are as follows:

Divisional chief accountant   £72.50
Assistant accountant   £38.00
Accounting technician (you)   £21.45
Secretary   £17.30

The spreadsheet needs to show the hours spent and costs per person, by week, for a three-week assignment. The time spent each week is shown below:

	Week 3	*Week 2*	*Week 1*
Divisional chief accountant	6 hrs 45 mins	4 hrs 30 mins	–
Assistant accountant	35 hrs	40 hrs	20 hrs
You	37 hrs 30 mins	40 hrs	32 hrs
Secretary	37 hrs 15 mins	32 hrs 15 mins	15 hrs

Setting up the assumptions area

As we will be referring to the chargeout rates for each week's costs, set these up in a separate area of the spreadsheet.

Headings and layout

Next we will enter the various **headings** required.

You want your spreadsheet to look like this:

	A	B	C	D	E	F	G
1	**Internal chargeout rates**						
2	Divisional chief accountant	£72.50					
3	Assistant accountant	£38.00					
4	Accounting technician	£21.45					
5	Secretary	£17.30					
6							
7	**Costs**	*Week 1*	*Week 2*	*Week 3*	Total		
8	Divisional chief accountant						
9	Assistant accountant						
10	Accounting technician						
11	Secretary						
12	**Total**						
13							
14	**Hours**	*Week 1*	*Week 2*	*Week 3*	Total		
15	Divisional chief accountant						
16	Assistant accountant						
17	Accounting technician						
18	Secretary						
19	**Total**						

Note the following points.

(a) Column A is wider to allow longer items of text to be entered. Depending on how your copy of Excel is set up, this might happen automatically or you may have to drag the line between the A and B columns to the right.

(b) We have used a **simple style for headings**. Headings tell users what data relates to and what the spreadsheet 'does'. We have made some words **bold**.

(c) **Numbers** should be **right-aligned** in cells. This usually happens automatically when you enter a number into a cell.

(d) We have left **spaces** in certain rows (after blocks of related items) to make the spreadsheet **easier to use and read**.

(e) Totals have been highlighted by a single line above and a double line below. This can be done by highlighting the relevant cells, then going to the **Styles** group in the **Home** section of the Ribbon, clicking on the drop-down arrow and choosing the style you want – in this case, '**Totals**'.

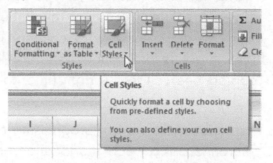

Alternatively, highlight the relevant cells, go to the **Font** area of the **Home** section and click on the drop-down arrow to access the list of **borders** available:

Entering data

Enter the time data in cells B15 to D18. Make sure you enter it correctly – the data is given to you in the order week 3 to week 1, but you would prefer it to be in the order week 1 to week 3. You will need to convert the time to decimal numbers.

	Week 1	Week 2	Week 3	Total
14 Hours				
15 Divisional chief accountant	0	4.5	6.75	
16 Assistant accountant	20	40	35	
17 Accounting technician	32	40	37.5	
18 Secretary	15	32.25	37.25	
19 Total				(Ctrl) ▾

Inserting formulas

The next step is to enter the **formulas** required. For example, in cell B19 you want the total hours for Week 1. In cell B8 you want the total cost of time spent. You could enter this formula as =B15*B2, but you need to make sure that, as you copy the formula across for Weeks 2 and 3, you still refer to the chargeout rate in B2.

The quick way to insert a series of formulas is to type in the initial one and then to copy across a row or down a column. You may remember that cell references are cleverly updated as you move along the row or column. This was called **relative copying**. However, that will get us into trouble here. If cell B8 contains the formula =B15*B2 and that is copied one cell to the right (into column C), the formula will become =C15*C2.

The C15 reference is correct because we are progressing along the row, one month at a time, but the C2 reference is incorrect. The location of the chargeout rate does not move: it is **absolute**. To prevent a cell reference being updated during the copying process put a '**$**' sign in front of the row and/or column reference.

A reference such as $A1 will mean that column A is always referred to as you copy across the spreadsheet. If you were to copy down, the references would be updated to A2, A3, A4, etc.

A reference such as A$1 will mean that row 1 is always referred to as you copy down the spreadsheet. If you were to copy across, the references would be updated to B1, C1, D1, etc.

A reference such as $A$1 will mean that cell A1 is always referred to no matter what copying of the formula is carried out.

The **function key F4** adds dollar signs to the cell reference, cycling through one, two or no dollar signs. Press the **F4** key as you are entering the cell address.

You should end up with the following figures:

B8		f_x =B15*$B$2				
	A	B	C	D	E	F	G
1	**Internal chargeout rates**						
2	Divisional chief accountant	£72.50					
3	Assistant accountant	£38.00					
4	Accounting technician	£21.45					
5	Secretary	£17.30					
6							
7	**Costs**	*Week 1*	*Week 2*	*Week 3*	*Total*		
8	Divisional chief accountant	0	326.25	489.375			
9	Assistant accountant	760	1520	1330			
10	Accounting technician	686.4	858	804.375			
11	Secretary	259.5	557.925	644.425			
12	**Total**						
13							
14	**Hours**	Week 1	Week 2	Week 3	Total		
15	Divisional chief accountant	0	4.5	6.75			
16	Assistant accountant	20	40	35			
17	Accounting technician	32	40	37.5			
18	Secretary	15	32.25	37.25			
19	**Total**						
20							
21							
22							
23							

Note that the formula in B8 refers to cell B15 (Week 1 hours) but to cell $B$2 – the absolute address of the chargeout rate.

The sales figures are untidy: some have comma separators between the thousands, some have one decimal place, some two. To tidy this up we will use the **Number** section of the Ribbon to format these numbers as **Currency**, and for the required **Decimal places** (two decimal places in this example). It is good practice to also format our results using **1000 separators**.

This drop-down provides more options, and is used in this example

(1) Select the range of cells B8:E12.

(2) Click in the small arrow, just right of the word **Number**, to open the **Format Cells** window.

(3) Select **Currency**; make sure the **Decimal places** reads 2 and that the £ symbol is showing.

   You should see that all the figures in your spreadsheet are now in the same format.

(4) In cell E8, enter a formula to total the hours.

The spreadsheet should now be like this:

	B8	▼	ƒx	=B15*$B$2		
	A	B	C	D	E	F
1	**Internal chargeout rates**					
2	Divisional chief accountant	£72.50				
3	Assistant accountant	£38.00				
4	Accounting technician	£21.45				
5	Secretary	£17.30				
6						
7	Costs	*Week 1*	*Week 2*	*Week 3*	*Total*	
8	Divisional chief accountant	£0.00	£326.25	£489.38	£815.63	
9	Assistant accountant	£760.00	£1,520.00	£1,330.00	£3,610.00	
10	Accounting technician	£686.40	£858.00	£804.38	£2,348.78	
11	Secretary	£259.50	£557.93	£644.43	£1,461.85	
12	**Total**	**£1,705.90**	**£3,262.18**	**£3,268.18**	**£8,236.25**	
13						
14	**Hours**	Week 1	Week 2	Week 3	Total	
15	Divisional chief accountant	0	4.5	6.75	11.25	
16	Assistant accountant	20	40	35	95	
17	Accounting technician	32	40	37.5	109.5	
18	Secretary	15	32.25	37.25	84.5	
19	**Total**	**67**	**116.75**	**116.5**	**300.25**	
20						
21						
22						

And the formulas behind the cell contents should be:

	A	B (Week 1)	C (Week 2)	D (Week 3)	E (Total)
6					
7	Costs	*Week 1*	*Week 2*	*Week 3*	*Total*
8	Divisional chief accountant	=B15*$B$2	=C15*$B$2	=D15*$B$2	=SUM(B8:D8)
9	Assistant accountant	=B16*$B$3	=C16*$B$3	=D16*$B$3	=SUM(B9:D9)
10	Accounting technician	=B17*$B$4	=C17*$B$4	=D17*$B$4	=SUM(B10:D10)
11	Secretary	=B18*$B$5	=C18*$B$5	=D18*$B$5	=SUM(B11:D11)
12	Total	=SUM(B8:B11)	=SUM(C8:C11)	=SUM(D8:D11)	=SUM(E8:E11)
13					
14	Hours	Week 1	Week 2	Week 3	Total
15	Divisional chief accountant	0	4.5	6.75	=SUM(B15:D15)
16	Assistant accountant	20	40	35	=SUM(B16:D16)
17	Accounting technician	32	40	37.5	=SUM(B17:D17)
18	Secretary	15	32.25	37.25	=SUM(B18:D18)
19	Total	=SUM(B15:B18)	=SUM(C15:C18)	=SUM(D15:D18)	=SUM(E15:E18)
20					
21					
22					

However, after designing the spreadsheet, you find out that the Divisional Chief Accountant has worked for 6 hours in week 4. He also wants you to add in to your calculations the costs of using two laptop computers which were charged out at £100 per week each, for the first 3 weeks. You have also found out that the secretarial chargeout rate was increased by 10% in week 3. You now need to amend the spreadsheet to reflect these changes.

(1) Insert a column between columns D and E.

(2) Label E7 and E14 as Week 4.

(3) Enter the 6 hours in cell E15.

(4) Enter a formula in cell E8 to calculate the cost of these hours.

(5) Insert a row between rows 11 and 12.

(6) Enter Laptops in cells A6 and A12.

(7) In cell A22, enter Laptops and enter the number of laptops used each week.

(8) In cell B6 enter the cost of each laptop per week.

(9) Use a formula in cells B12 to D12 to calculate the cost of the laptops.

(10) Insert two rows between row 6 and 7.

(11) In cell B7, enter the percentage increase in the secretary's chargeout rate. Format this cell as percentage. Amend the formula in cell D13 accordingly.

(12) You may have noticed that the total cost and total hours total have not altered. This is because we have inserted rows and columns which were outside the range of the original formula used to calculate the totals. Amend your formulas accordingly.

Tidy the spreadsheet

The presentation is reasonable as we have taken care of it as we have developed the spreadsheet. This is good practice. You can now apply different formatting techniques – changing font colour or cell colour, for example. To change font colour, type (eg Arial) and size including **cell fill colour** or shading go to **Home>Font**.

The menu extract below indicates the **font type** is Calibri, and is in size 11. The **cell fill colour** icon is similar in appearance to a paint pot. The **font colour** can be changed by the drop down menu in the 'A' next to the cell fill colour icon.

Once you have tidied up your spreadsheet save the spreadsheet as 'Costing Exercise-finished'.

The spreadsheet should now look like this before updating cell F22 to include the Divisional chief accountant's week 4 hours:

	F15		f_x	=SUM(F10:F14)			
	A	B	C	D	E	F	G
1	**Internal chargeout rates**						
2	Divisional chief accountant	£72.50					
3	Assistant accountant	£38.00					
4	Accounting technician	£21.45					
5	Secretary	£17.30					
6	Laptop cost	£100.00					
7	Chargeout rate	10%					
8							
9	Costs	*Week 1*	*Week 2*	*Week 3*	*Week 4*	*Total*	
10	Divisional chief accountant	£0.00	£326.25	£489.38	£435.00	£1,250.63	
11	Assistant accountant	£760.00	£1,520.00	£1,330.00	£0.00	£3,610.00	
12	Accounting technician	£686.40	£858.00	£804.38	£0.00	£2,348.78	
13	Secretary	£259.50	£557.93	£708.87	£0.00	£1,526.29	
14	Laptops	£200.00	£200.00	£200.00		£600.00	
15	**Total**	**£1,705.90**	**£3,262.18**	**£3,332.62**	**£435.00**	**£9,335.69**	
16							
17	**Hours**	Week 1	Week 2	Week 3	Week 4	Total	
18	Divisional chief accountant		4.5	6.75	6	17.25	
19	Assistant accountant	20	40	35		95	
20	Accounting technician	32	40	37.5		109.5	
21	Secretary	15	32.25	37.25		84.5	
22	Total	**67**	**116.75**	**116.5**	**6**	**300.25**	
23							
24	Laptops	2	2	2			
25							
26							
27							

And the formulas should look like this:

	F15		f_x	=SUM(F10:F14)		
	A	B	C	D	E	F
1	**Internal chargeout rates**					
2	Divisional chief accountant	72.5				
3	Assistant accountant	38				
4	Accounting technician	21.45				
5	Secretary	17.3				
6	Laptop cost	100				
7	Chargeout rate	0.1				
8						
9	Costs	*Week 1*	*Week 2*	*Week 3*	*Week 4*	*Total*
10	Divisional chief accountant	=B18*$B$2	=C18*$B$2	=D18*$B$2	=E18*$B$2	=SUM(B10:E10)
11	Assistant accountant	=B19*$B$3	=C19*$B$3	=D19*$B$3	=E19*$B$2	=SUM(B11:E11)
12	Accounting technician	=B20*$B$4	=C20*$B$4	=D20*$B$4	=E20*$B$2	=SUM(B12:E12)
13	Secretary	=B21*$B$5	=C21*$B$5	=D21*($B$5+($B$5*$	=E21*$B$2	=SUM(B13:E13)
14	Laptops	=B24*$B$6	=C24*$B$6	=D24*$B$6		=SUM(B14:E14)
15	**Total**	=SUM(B10:B13)	=SUM(C10:C13)	=SUM(D10:D13)	=SUM(E10:E13)	=SUM(F10:F14)
16						
17	**Hours**	Week 1	Week 2	Week 3	Week 4	Total
18	Divisional chief accountant		4.5	6.75	6	=SUM(B18:E18)
19	Assistant accountant	20	40	35		=SUM(B19:D19)
20	Accounting technician	32	40	37.5		=SUM(B20:D20)
21	Secretary	15	32.25	37.25		=SUM(B21:D21)
22	Total	=SUM(B18:B21)	=SUM(C18:C21)	=SUM(D18:D21)	=SUM(E18:E21)	=SUM(B22:D22)
23						
24	Laptops	2	2	2		
25						
26						
27						
28						

Illustration 8: Commission calculations

Commission calculations.

Four telesales staff each earn a basic salary of £14,000 pa. They also earn a commission of 2% of sales. The following spreadsheet has been created to process their commission and total earnings. **Give an appropriate formula for each of the following cells.**

(a) Cell D4

(b) Cell E6

(c) Cell D9

(d) Cell E9

	A	B	C	D	E
1	Sales team salaries and commissions – 200X				
2	Name	Sales	Salary	Commission	Total earnings
3		£	£	£	£
4	Northington	284,000	14,000	5,680	19,680
5	Souther	193,000	14,000	3,860	17,860
6	Weston	12,000	14,000	240	14,240
7	Easterman	152,000	14,000	3,040	17,040
8					
9	Total	641,000	56,000	12,820	68,820
10					
11					
12	Variables				
13	Basic Salary	14,000			
14	Commission rate	0.02			
15					

Solution

Possible formulas are:

(a) =B4*$B$14

(b) =C6+D6

(c) =SUM(D4:D7)

(d) There are a number of possibilities here, depending on whether you set the cell as the total of the earnings of each salesman (cells E4 to E7): =SUM(E4:E7) or as the total of the different elements of remuneration (cells C9 and D9): =SUM(C9:D9). Even better would be a formula that checked that both calculations gave the same answer. A suitable formula for this purpose would be:

=IF(SUM(E4:E7)=SUM(C9:D9),SUM(E4:E7),"ERROR")

We explain this formula after the next illustration, so don't worry about it at the moment!

Illustration 9: Actual sales and budgeted sales

Actual sales compared with budget sales.

A business often compares its results against budgets or targets. It is useful to express differences or **variations as a percentage of the original budget**, for example sales may be 10% higher than predicted.

Continuing the telesales example, a spreadsheet could be set up as follows, showing differences between actual sales and target sales, and expressing the difference as a percentage of target sales.

	A	B	C	D	E
1	Sales team comparison of actual against budget sales				
2	Name	Sales (Budget)	Sales (Actual)	Difference	% of budget
3		£	£	£	£
4	Northington	275,000	284,000	9,000	3.27
5	Souther	200,000	193,000	(7,000)	(3.50)
6	Weston	10,000	12,000	2,000	20.00
7	Easterman	153,000	152,000	(1,000)	(0.65)
8					
9	Total	638,000	641,000	3,000	0.47
10					

Give a suitable formula for each of the following cells.

(a) Cell D4

(b) Cell E6

(c) Cell E9

Try this for yourself, before looking at the solution.

Solution

(a) =C4-B4

(b) =(D6/B6)*100

(c) =(D9/B9)*100. Note that in (c) you **cannot simply add up the individual percentage differences**, as the percentages are based on different quantities

3 Formulas with conditions ('IF' function)

Suppose the employing company in the above example awards a bonus to people who exceed their target by more than £1,000. The spreadsheet could work out who is entitled to the bonus.

To do this we would enter the appropriate formula in cells F4 to F7. For salesperson Easterman, we would enter the following in cell F7:

=IF(D4>1000,"BONUS"," ")

We will now explain this **IF** function.

IF statements follow the following structure (or 'syntax').

=IF(logical_test, value_if_true, value_if_false)

The **logical_test** is any value or expression that can be evaluated to Yes or No. For example, D4>1000 is a logical expression; if the value in cell D4 is over 1,000, the expression evaluates to Yes. Otherwise, the expression evaluates to No.

Value_if_true is the value that is returned if the answer to the **logical_test** is Yes. For example, if the answer to D4>1000 is Yes, and the **value_if_true** is the text string "BONUS", then the cell containing the IF function will display the text "BONUS".

Value_if_false is the value that is returned if the answer to the **logical_test** is No. For example, if the **value_if_false** is two sets of quote marks " " this means display a blank cell if the answer to the **logical_test** is No. So, in our example, if D4 is not over 1,000, then the cell containing the IF function will display a blank cell.

Note the following symbols which can be used in formulas with conditions:

<	less than
<=	less than or equal to
=	equal to
>=	greater than or equal to
>	greater than
<>	not equal to

Care is required to ensure **brackets** and **commas** are entered in the right places. If, when you try out this kind of formula, you get an error message, it may well be a simple mistake, such as leaving a comma or bracket out.

Illustration 10: The IF function

Using the **IF** function.

A company offers a discount of 5% to customers who order more than £10,000 worth of goods. A spreadsheet showing what customers will pay may look like:

C8			f_x	=IF(B8>$C$3, B8*$C$4,0)	
	A	B	C	D	E	F
1	**Sales discount**					
2						
3	Discount hurdle		10,000			
4	Discount rate		5%			
5						
6	Customer	Sales	Discount	Net price		
7		£	£	£		
8	John	12,000	600	11,400		
9	Margaret	9,000	0	9,000		
10	William	8,000	0	8,000		
11	Julie	20,000	1000	19,000		
12						
13						
14						
15						

The formula in cell C8 is as shown: =**IF**(B8>$C$3, B8*$C$4, 0). This means, if the value in B8 is greater than £10,000 multiply it by the contents of C4, ie 5%, otherwise the discount will be zero. Cell D8 will calculate the amount net of discount, using the formula =B8–C8. The same conditional formula, with the cell references changed, will be found in cells C9, C10 and C11.

Here is another illustration for you to try.

Illustration 11: The IF function

Open the spreadsheet called 'Exam Results' (one of the spreadsheets downloaded from https://learningmedia.bpp.com/catalog?pagename=AAT_Spreadsheets).

There are ten candidates listed, together with their marks.

The pass mark has been set at 50%.

See if you can complete column C, rows 6 – 15, so that it shows PASS if the candidate scores 50 or above, and FAIL if the candidate scores less than 50.

Once it's set up and working correctly, change the pass mark in cell B3 to 60 and ensure that the PASS/FAIL indications reflect the change.

The formulas you need will be based on the one for cell C6.

| C6 | | f_x | =IF(B6>=$B$3, "PASS","FAIL") |

Book3

	A	B	C	D	E	F
1	**Exam results**					
2						
3	Pass mark	50				
4						
5	**Candidate**	**Mark**	**Pass/fail**			
6	Alf	51	PASS			
7	Beth	56	PASS			
8	Charles	82	PASS			
9	David	42	FAIL			
10	Edwina	68	PASS			
11	Frances	36	FAIL			
12	Gary	75	PASS			
13	Hugh	53	PASS			
14	Iris	72	PASS			
15	John	34	FAIL			

Countif

The countif formula can be used to **count** how many cell values meet a specific criteria **IF** a condition is met.

Counta

The counta formula can be used to count the number of cells in a range that are not empty, and do hold a value. Bear in mind that although a cell may appear blank technically it may not be empty as may contain a non-visible value.

The cells below in A1, A2 and A3 hold a non-visible value (apostrophes in this case) so there are three cells that are not empty.

The following **counta** formula will give the correct count of **3**.

	A
1	
2	
3	
4	=COUNTA(A1:A3)

Assessment focus point

In the assessment you may be asked to analyse and interpret data, including using forecasting tools. Make sure you understand how the different tools can be used and the most appropriate uses for them.

For example, our business in the above example may wish to know how many times sales have exceeded £10,000.

The answer here is twice, or **2** as both £12,000 and £14,000 are over £10,000. The following countif formula would calculate **2** as the result.

	A	B
1		**Sales £**
2	**Week 1**	8000
3	**Week 2**	12000
4	**Week 3**	9000
5	**Week 4**	14000
6		=COUNTIF(B2:B5,">10,000")

Compound (nested) IF functions

IF functions can also have multiple conditions within a formula meaning that two or more conditions need to be met for the calculation.

For example, a business may wish to give a 5% discount to customers who have made a sales order between £500 and £1,000. Here the **IF** function used would

need to include two conditions for '>500' and '<1,000' and also be able to calculate the value of the 5% discount.

The following customers have made the following orders:

	A	B	C
1	**Customer**	**Order £**	**Discount £**
2	Cerise plc	450	
3	Green Ltd	800	
4	Plum Partners	1060	
5	Violet Ltd	900	

To calculate the discounts in column C the following **IF** formulas can be used:

	A	B	C
1	**Customer**	**Order £**	**Discount £**
2	Cerise plc	450	=IF((B2>500),(B2<1000))*B2*0.05
3	Green Ltd	800	=IF((B3>500),(B3<1000))*B3*0.05
4	Plum Partners	1060	=IF((B4>500),(B4<1000))*B4*0.05
5	Violet Ltd	900	=IF((B5>500),(B5<1000))*B5*0.05

To give the following results:

	A	B	C
1	**Customer**	**Order £**	**Discount £**
2	Cerise plc	450	0
3	Green Ltd	800	40
4	Plum Partners	1060	0
5	Violet Ltd	900	45

Note how two conditions have been included in one formula and these have to be met before the discount of 5% applies.

Assessment focus point

You may need to use a combination of different formulas to achieve an object set in the assessment so be flexible and imaginative in how you can apply your spreadsheets skills. For example, in the above worksheet an **IF** Function can be used in column C to calculate discounts and also a **SUM** formula to total the order values in column B.

3.1 Conditional formatting

In addition to the condition determining whether PASS or FAIL appears, you can also conditionally format cell contents – for example, by altering the colour of a cell to highlight problems. This can be done by accessing the **Conditional Formatting** option in the **Styles** section of the **Home** tab of the Ribbon.

The marks which are less than the value in B3 have been highlighted by making the cell background red and the text white, as illustrated below:

	A	B	C
1	**Exam results**		
2			
3	Pass mark	50	
4			
5	**Candidate**	**Mark**	**Pass/fail**
6	Alf	51	PASS
7	Beth	56	PASS
8	Charles	82	PASS
9	David	42	FAIL
10	Edwina	68	PASS
11	Frances	36	FAIL
12	Gary	75	PASS
13	Hugh	53	PASS
14	Iris	72	PASS
15	John	34	FAIL

To produce the above result:

(1) Change the pass mark back to 50% if it is still at 60%.

(2) Highlight the numbers in column B.

(3) Click **Conditional formatting>Highlight cell rules>Less than**. You will see there are two white entry boxes.

(4) Click on cell B3. This will be entered automatically into the first box.

(5) Then click on the down arrow next to the second entry box. Click on **Custom format>Fill** and choose the red box. This changes the colour of the cell.

(6) Then click on **Font** and click the down arrow next to **Automatic**, under **Colour**, and choose the white box.

(7) Click **OK**.

You can also use Conditional formatting to highlight the top three results, for example:

	A	B	C	D
1	**Exam results**			
2				
3	Pass mark	50		
4				
5	**Candidate**	**Mark**	**Pass/fail**	
6	Alf	51	PASS	
7	Beth	56	PASS	
8	Charles	82	PASS	
9	David	42	FAIL	
10	Edwina	68	PASS	
11	Frances	36	FAIL	
12	Gary	75	PASS	
13	Hugh	53	PASS	
14	Iris	72	PASS	
15	John	34	FAIL	
16				
17				
18				
19				
20				

To produce the above result:

(1) Highlight the numbers in column B.

(2) Click **Conditional formatting>Top/Bottom rules>Top 10 items.**

(3) In the first entry box, change the number from 10 to 3.

(4) In the second entry box, click on **Custom format>Fill** and choose the green box. This changes the colour of the cell.

(5) Then click on **Font** and click the down arrow next to **Automatic**, under **Colour** and choose the white box.

(6) Click **OK**.

3.2 Ranking data

Assessment focus point

Your skill requirement of ranking data is purely to have knowledge that it can be performed. You will not be asked to rank data in your live assessment.

The **RANK** function, one of Excel's statistical functions, ranks a number compared to other numbers in a list of data.

The syntax for the RANK function is:

= RANK (Number, Ref, Order)

Number – the cell reference of the number to be ranked.

Ref – the range of cells to use in ranking the Number.

Order – determines whether the Number is ranked in ascending or descending order. Use 0 for descending order and 1 for ascending order.

The names in the 'Exam Results' spreadsheet are in alphabetical order. Say you want to keep them in that order but you want to see who came first, second, third etc. You can use RANK to give that information.

	D6			f_x	=RANK(B6,$B$6:$B$15,0)		
	A	B	C	D	E	F	G
1	Exam results						
2							
3	Pass mark	50					
4							
5	Candidate	Mark	Pass/fail	Rank			
6	Alf	51	PASS	7			
7	Beth	56	PASS	5			
8	Charles	82	PASS	1			
9	David	42	FAIL	8			
10	Edwina	68	PASS	4			
11	Frances	36	FAIL	9			
12	Gary	75	PASS	2			
13	Hugh	53	PASS	6			
14	Iris	72	PASS	3			
15	John	34	FAIL	10			
16							
17							

To produce the above result:

(1) Enter Rank in cell D5.

(2) In cell D6, type =RANK(B6,$B$6:$B$15,0). This means that B6 will be ranked within the range B6:B15 in descending order.

(3) Copy the formula to cells B7 to B15.

4 Charts and graphs

Charts and graphs are useful and powerful ways of communicating trends and relative sizes of numerical data in various output to meet equality of opportunity for users. Excel makes the production of charts relatively easy through the use of the chart wizard.

We will use the 'Sales discount' spreadsheet (one of the spreadsheets downloaded from https://learningmedia.bpp.com/catalog?pagename=AAT_Spreadsheets) to generate a number of different charts.

	A	B	C	D
1	**Sales discount**			
2				
3	Discount hurdle		10,000	
4	Discount rate		5%	
5				
6	Customer	Sales	Discount	Net price
7		£	£	£
8	John	12,000	600	11,400
9	Margaret	9,000	0	9,000
10	William	8,000	0	8,000
11	Julie	20,000	1000	19,000

First, we will generate a simple pie chart showing the total sales figure, before discounts.

Illustration 12: Pie charts

(1) Open the 'Sales discount' spreadsheet.

(2) Place your cursor on the word 'Customer', hold down the mouse button and drag the cursor downwards until you have selected the four names and four sales figures.

(3) Select the **Insert** section from the Ribbon, then **Pie>3-D pie**.

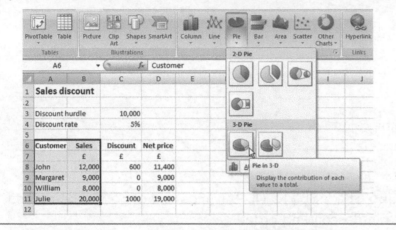

This will generate a pie chart that looks like this:

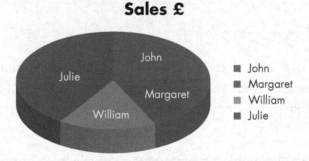

You will see that it already has a title, 'Sales £'. To make any changes to this, double-click the area where the title appears, then enter additional text or delete text you do not want. Below we have added 'for 20XX' and brackets around the pound sign.

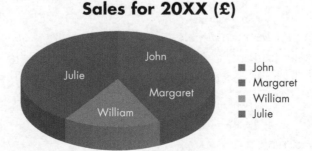

Changing the chart type

If you decide that a different chart may be more suitable for presenting your data you can easily change the chart type.

(1) Click on your chart. The **Chart Tools** options should become available at the top of the window.

(2) Click **Design>Change Chart Type**.

(3) From here, pick some charts from the following chart types to see what they produce: **3D**, **Bar**, **Column**, **Exploded**, **Line and Stacked**. For example, the stacked chart will produce something like this:

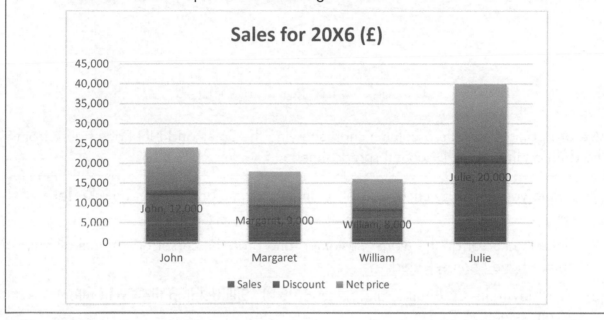

Bar charts

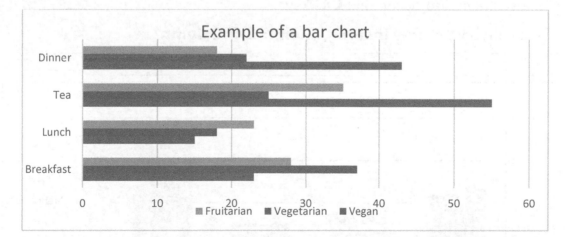

A pie chart is good for showing relative sizes of elements making up a total. However, sometimes you may want to be able to compare how two series of data are moving: sales and gross profit, for example. In this case, bar charts (or line charts) are more suitable. Excel makes a distinction between bar charts that show vertical bars and those that show horizontal bars.

When the data is shown vertically Excel refers to the chart as a 'column' chart; whereas if the data is shown horizontally it is a 'bar' chart.

Line chart

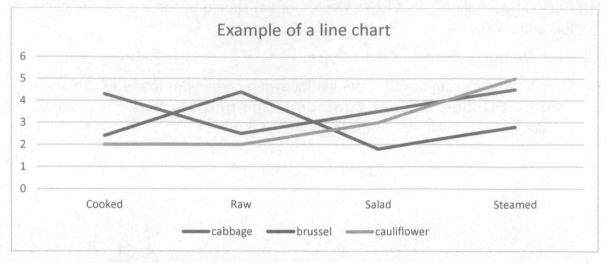

We are going to create a column chart showing the Sales and Net Price figure from the data on the 'Sales Discount' spreadsheet.

(1) Delete your chart by clicking on its outermost frame and pressing the **Delete** key.

(2) Place the cursor on the word 'Customer' and drag the cursor down until all four names have been selected.

(3) Hold down the **Ctrl** button and select B6:B11. Still holding the **Ctrl** button down, select D6:D11.

(4) Release the mouse button and **Ctrl** key.

(5) On the Ribbon, choose **Insert>Column>2-D Column**.

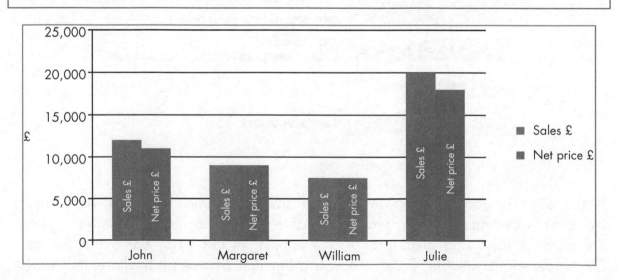

This time there is no automatic chart title, so we will need to add one.

Click on the chart. At the top of the window you will see **Chart Tools** appear:

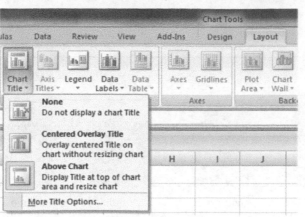

From the **Layout** section, choose **Labels>Chart Title>Above Chart**.

Type in 'Sales and Net Prices for 20XX (£)'.

To the right of the chart you will see a description for each column. This is called a Legend. You can move the legend by clicking on the **Legend** button.

You should also label the horizontal axis and the vertical axis.

(1) To label the horizontal axis, click **Layout>Axis Titles>Primary Horizontal Axis>Title below axis** (make sure you are clicked on the chart to see the **Chart Tools** tabs).

(2) The words 'Axis Title' appear at the bottom of the chart. Click on this, then press **Ctrl + A** to select all the words and type in your axis title, in this case 'Customer'.

(3) To label the other axis, this time choose **Primary Vertical Axis**. You have a choice of directions for your text. Choose **Horizontal Title** and type a pound sign.

Note that, if you are typing words for the vertical axis title, the best option is usually **Rotated Title**. Try experimenting with that now.

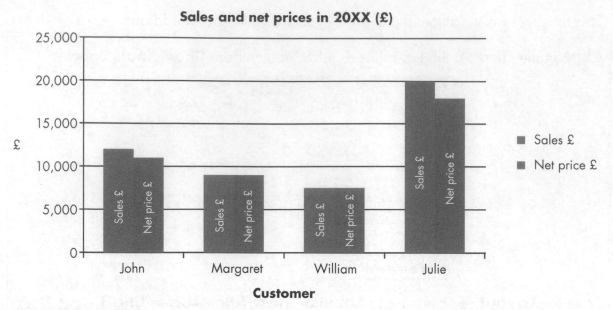

Sales and net prices in 20XX (£)

Exploded charts

These are useful when you want to highlight key areas of data within the chart itself

Using the spreadsheet 'Sales discount'

---

(1) Highlight the data to create a pie chart (cells A6:B11), click on **Insert>Charts** (you may have a **Recommended Charts** icon or a **pie chart icon**, either will work, you are aiming to create a pie chart initially)

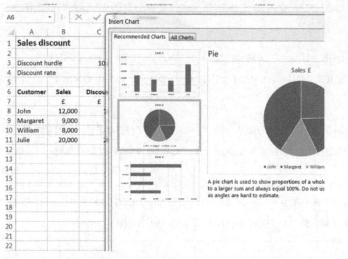

(2) Click OK to accept the pie chart option.

(3) Right click to see the options and select **Format Chart Area**, and the options will open on the right hand side of the screen. Click on **Chart Options** drop down box will offer a fresh set of options, including **Series Sales £.**

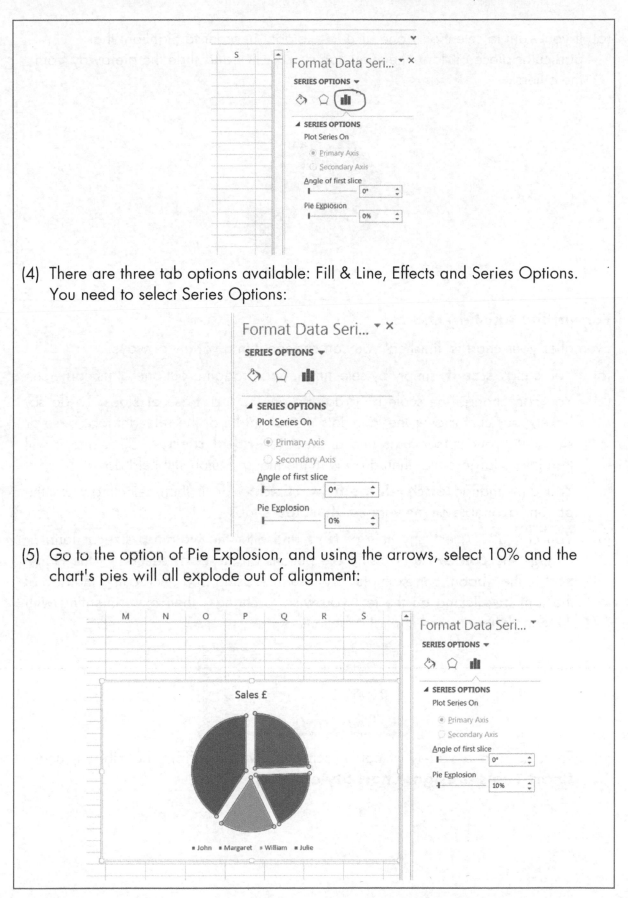

(4) There are three tab options available: Fill & Line, Effects and Series Options. You need to select Series Options:

(5) Go to the option of Pie Explosion, and using the arrows, select 10% and the chart's pies will all explode out of alignment:

(6) If you want to select only one slice to explode, in order to highlight that particular piece of data, then you can simply click and slide the pie away from the others:

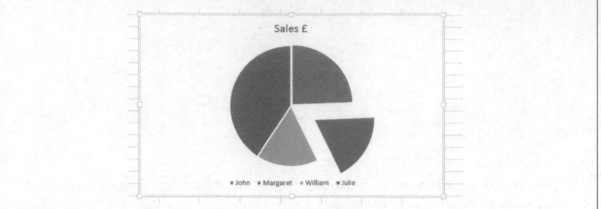

Sales £

■ John ■ Margaret ■ William ■ Julie

Formatting existing charts

Even after your chart is 'finished' you can change it in a variety of ways.

(a) You can **resize it**, simply by selecting it and dragging out one of its corners.

(b) You can change the scale by dragging out the top, base or sides. To do so, hover your cursor over the four dots in the middle of the relevant top, base or side until your cursor turns into a **double-ended arrow**. Click and it will turn into a large cross, then drag with the mouse button still held down.

(c) You can change **each element** by **clicking** on it then selecting from the options available on the various **Chart tools** tabs.

(d) You can also select any item of **text** and alter the wording, size or font; or change the **colours** used using the buttons on the **Font** section of the Home part of the ribbon. For example, practise increasing and decreasing the size of the font by clicking on the text you wish to change, then experimenting with the two different-sized capital A buttons:

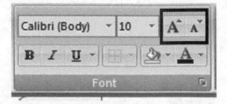

(e) There is also a variety of colour schemes available from the Ribbon, under **Chart Tools>Design>Chart Styles.**

Assessment focus point

In the assessment you may need to move your chart to a specified location on the worksheet. For example, perhaps to the right or below the source data. To move your chart, hover your mouse cursor over one of the four corners of the chart and move as required.

To move a chart to a new worksheet select **Chart Tools**, then **Design** and then **Move Chart**.

Simple data manipulation

Illustration 13: Data manipulation

A database can be viewed simply as a collection of data. There is a simple database related to inventory, called 'Stockman Ltd', within the files downloaded from https://learningmedia.bpp.com/catalog?pagename=AAT_Spreadsheets. Open it now.

There are a number of features worth pointing out in this spreadsheet before we start data manipulation.

(1) Each row from 4–15 holds an inventory record.

(2) Column G makes use of the **IF** function to determine if the inventory needs to be reordered (when quantity < reorder level).

(3) In row 2, the spreadsheet uses automatic word wrap within some cells. This can improve presentation if there are long descriptions. To use word wrap, select the cells you want it to apply to, then click the **Wrap Text** icon in the **Alignment** section of the **Home** tab. The height of the cells needs to be increased to accommodate more than one line of text. To do this, select the whole row, then double-click on the line between the row numbers 2 and 3; or, instead, select **AutoFit Row Height** as shown below.

The data is currently arranged in part number order.

Wrap text in cell   AutoFit Row Height

	A	B	C	D	E	F	G	H	I
1	**Stockman Ltd**								
2	Part code	Supplier	Quantity	Reorder level	Unit price	Value	Order needed		
3					£	£			
4	129394	A Ltd	124	100	20	2,480.00	Yes		
5	129395	B Ltd	4325	4500	14	60,550.00			
6	129396	F Ltd	4626	4000	12	55,512.00			
7	129397	A Ltd	583	500	14	8,162.00	Yes		
8	129398	D Ltd	43	50	37	1,591.00	Yes		
9	129399	E Ltd	837	1000	65	54,405.00			
10	129400	B Ltd	84	50	34	2,856.00	Yes		
11	129401	F Ltd	4847	5000	20	96,940.00			
12	129402	D Ltd	4632	4000	10	46,320.00			
13	129403	A Ltd	41	40	34	1,394.00			
14	129404	E Ltd	5578	5000	25	139,450.00	Yes		
15	129405	C Ltd	5	10	35	175.00			
16					Total	469,835.00			
17									
18									
19									
20									

The horizontal rows are records: one record for each inventory type. The vertical columns are attributes (qualities) relating to each record.

Sorting the data

Let's say that we want to sort the data into descending value order.

(1) Select the data range A4:G15.

(2) At the right-hand side of the **Home** section of the Ribbon (and in the **Data** section of the Ribbon) you will see the **Sort & Filter** drop-down menu.

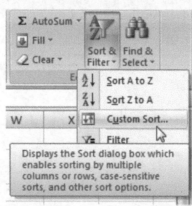

(3) Choose **Custom Sort**.

(4) Sort by Column F, largest to smallest.

(5) Click **OK**.

You will see that the data has been sorted by value.

If you now **Sort by** Supplier (**Order A–Z**) you will have the data arranged by supplier, and within that by value.

Sorting with multiple criteria

You may wish to sort your data using two more criteria (rather than by one column in the illustration above).

To sort data using multiple criteria within **Custom Sort** select **Add Level** to add additional sort criteria.

| $^+_Z↓$ Add Level | ✕ Delete Level | 🖹 Copy Level | ▲ | ▼ | Options... |

Assessment focus point

You must be able to select the most appropriate chart or graph to summarise and present the information in the assessment. Remember to select tools such as labels, legends and the correct scale to answer the specific question. Being able to critically select and manipulate data is essential to success.

5 Printing

5.1 Printing spreadsheets

The print options for your spreadsheet may be accessed by selecting **File button** and **Print**, or pressing **Ctrl + P**. Printing large spreadsheets without checking the print and layout settings will often result in printouts spread messily over several pages.

It is a good idea to at least opt for **Print Preview**, to see what your printout will look like before printing.

A better option is to control what prints more precisely. This can be done from the **Page Layout** section of the Ribbon.

| Home | Insert | Page Layout | Formulas | Data | Review | View | Add-Ins |

This allows you to, for example, print out selected areas only, include/exclude gridlines and the column and row headings, alter the orientation of the page and so on.

Scaling for printing or publication

The **Scale to Fit** section within **Page Layout** allows a worksheet to be scaled to a required size for printing or publication. Changing **Automatic** to **1 page** will mean all the data on that worksheet will be sized to one page.

Illustration 14: Page layout and printing

Open the spreadsheet we saw earlier called 'Costing Exercise – Finished'.

Assume that we only want to print out the cash flow without the table at the top showing the assumptions. We want to show the gridlines, but not the A, B, C... or 1, 2, 3... that head up columns and rows.

(1) Select the range A9:F24.

(2) Choose **Page Layout>Print Area>Set Print Area** from the Ribbon.

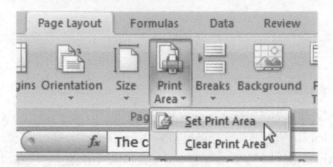

(3) Check the **Print Gridlines** box in **Page Layout>Sheet** options.

(4) Choose **Office Button>Print>Print Preview**.

At this point you can check for obvious layout and formatting errors.

Spelling

Before you print, it is wise to check your work for spelling mistakes. To do this click the **Review** tab and select **Spelling**. If you have made any spelling errors Excel will offer alternative **Suggestions** which you can accept by clicking **Change** or ignore by clicking **Ignore (Once** or **All).**

If the word is, in fact, correct (for example, terminology that Excel does not recognise) you can add it to Excel's dictionary by clicking **Add to Dictionary**.

Preparing your spreadsheet for printing: Page set-up

The **Page Setup** area of the **Page Layout** tab on the Ribbon also allows you to specify certain other details that affect how your spreadsheet looks when it prints out.

From here you can set the size of the **Margins** (the white spaces that print around the spreadsheet) and choose whether to print the spreadsheet in landscape **Orientation** (ie wider than tall) rather than the default portrait **Orientation** (taller than wide).

If you want to make sure that your spreadsheet will print onto one page, you can choose **Fit to** 1 page wide by 1 page tall. This can be done by accessing the **Page Setup** options, by clicking on the little arrow in the bottom-right corner of the section on the ribbon.

Imagine you are printing out a spreadsheet that will cover several pages. It is important that certain information is present on each page. For example:

- The spreadsheet title
- The page number and total pages
- The author
- The row and column headings

This can be done by accessing the **Page Setup** options, in the way outlined above, or by clicking on the **Print Titles** icon.

Headers appear at the top of each page. For example, a custom header could be:

Author   Budget for 2013   Date printed

Footers appear at the bottom of each page, for example:

Page   File name

The **Sheet** tab allows you to specify the rows and columns to be repeated on each page. For example, you might want to repeat the months across the top of each page and the type of income down the left of each page.

We have provided a demonstration spreadsheet in the downloaded files, 'Print practice'. Open it and try the following:

> Insert a **Header**: Author name, Title (Budget 2013) Date printed

> Insert a **Footer**: Page number, File name

Click **Page setup (or Print Titles)>Header/Footer> Custom Header** and **Custom Footer**.

Ensure that the headings in column A are repeated on the second page.

Use this spreadsheet to insert page breaks (**Breaks**) and other options in the **Page Setup** area to:

* Insert the current filename in the bottom centre of the page
* Ensure page numbers are inserted top right of the page
* Insert a date and time in the top left of the page

Assessment focus point

Always look out for instructions on the assessment for entering headers and footers and always enter using the appropriate information and the correct location on the page. Remember your audience in the preparation of any report, so consider using summary sheets, hiding unnecessary rows/columns and adding labels to ensure clarity. You will not be asked to insert page breaks or page numbers, but these are included to enhance your business knowledge of Excel.

Printing formulas

Occasionally, perhaps for documentation or checking, you might want the spreadsheet formulas to be printed out instead of the calculated results of the formula. To do this:

(1) Display the formulas on the screen by pressing **Ctrl + `** (or **Formulas** in the ribbon and **Show formulas**)

(2) Set the area you want to be printed: **Page Layout>Print Area>Set Area**

(3) Check what the printout will look like **Office button>Print>Print preview**

(4) Adjust as necessary and print out when happy with the display

Printing charts

Charts can be printed either with or without the data on the worksheet.

To print only the chart simply click on it and then press **Ctrl + P**. As always, it is wise to **Print Preview** first.

If you also want to print the worksheet data, click away from the chart into any cell. Use **Print Preview** to make sure that the chart is the right size and is in the right position. Then press **Ctrl + P**.

Annotating output

You may wish to add information to your spreadsheets by using **comment boxes** annotate worksheets. Comment boxes can be added through **Review>New Comment**. Comment boxes can also be hidden through the **Review** tab if you prefer your annotations to be out of sight.

Charts and graphs can be annotated by using **Text Boxes**. To use this technique select **Insert>Text>Text Box**. You can then drag your text box to any location on your chart or graph.

Chapter summary

- A **spreadsheet** is basically an electronic piece of paper divided into **rows** and **columns**. The intersection of a row and a column is known as a cell.

- Essential basic **skills** include how to **move around** within a spreadsheet, how to **enter** and **edit** data, how to **fill** cells, how to **insert** and **delete** columns and rows and how to improve the basic **layout** and **appearance** of a spreadsheet.

- **Relative** cell references (eg B3) change when you copy formulas to other locations or move data from one place to another. **Absolute** cell references (eg $B$3) stay the same.

- A wide range of **formulas** and functions are available within Excel. We looked at the use of conditional formulas that use an **IF** statement.

- A spreadsheet should be given a **title** which clearly defines its purpose. The contents of rows and columns should also be clearly **labelled**. **Formatting** should be used to make the data in the spreadsheet easy to read and interpret.

- **Numbers** can be **formatted** in several ways, for instance with commas, as percentages, as currency or with a certain number of decimal places.

- Excel includes the facility to produce a range of charts and graphs. The **Chart Wizard** provides a tool to simplify the process of chart construction.

- Spreadsheets can be **printed** and the **Print Preview** function can be used to see what a printout will look like before actually printing.

- Spreadsheets can be used in a variety of accounting contexts. You should practise using spreadsheets, as **hands-on experience** is the key to spreadsheet proficiency.

Keywords

- **Absolute (reference):** A cell reference that does not change and is particularly useful when copying a formula across data

- **Bar chart:** A chart where data is grouped into 'bars', customarily used to show relative size between groups

- **Conditional formatting:** Allows users to format cells depending on specified conditions

- **Copying and pasting formulas:** A technique using an existing formula to quickly apply to different cell references within a spreadsheet

- **Fill handle:** A black cursor sign **+** that indicates it is possible to drag the cursor to infill cells

- **Formulas:** Used in calculating a range of requested values

- **IF function:** A logical function that calculates a value or outcome depending on specified conditions

- **House style:** A standardised style of formatting adopted by organisations

- **Orientation:** Describes the style of presentation or printing set-up chosen, ie landscape or portrait

- **Page layout:** Allows users to print specific areas of a worksheet

- **Paste special:** Used when copying values instead of formulas

- **Pie chart:** A circular chart displaying segments of data

- **Print preview:** Allows users to see what the printout will look like before printing

- **Ranking data:** A statistical function that ranks or classifies the size of a number compared to other numbers in the same list

- **Relative copying:** A cell reference that does change when copying a formula across data

- **Summary sheet:** A worksheet that links to other data or worksheets

- **Workbook:** A spreadsheet that consists of one or more worksheets

- **Worksheet:** Individual spreadsheet pages contained in a workbook

1 **List three types of cell contents.**

2 **What do the F5 and F2 keys do in Excel?**

3 **What technique can you use to insert a logical series of data such as 1, 2 .... 10, or Jan, Feb, March etc?**

4 **How do you display formulas instead of the results of formulas in a spreadsheet?**

5 **List five possible changes that may improve the appearance of a spreadsheet.**

6 **What is the syntax (pattern) of an IF function in Excel?**

7 The following spreadsheet shows sales of two products, the Ego and the Id, for the period July to September.

	A	B	C	D	E
1	Sigmund Ltd				
2	Sales analysis - quarter 3, 2010				
3		July	August	September	Total
4	Ego	3,000	4,000	2,000	9,000
5	Id	2,000	1,500	4,000	7,500
6	Total	5,000	5,500	6,000	16,500
7					

Devise a suitable formula for each of the following cells.

(a) Cell B6

(b) Cell E5

(c) Cell E6

8 The following spreadsheet shows sales, exclusive of VAT, the VAT amounts and the VAT inclusive amounts. The old VAT rate of 17.5% has been used and needs to be updated to the new 20% rate. It is important that this can easily be changed without needing to change any of the formulas in the spreadsheet.

	A	B	C	D
1	Taxable Supplies Ltd		Vat rate	0.175
2				
3		January	February	March
4	Product A	5,000	4,000	3,000
5	Product B	2,000	1,500	4,000
6	Product C	7,000	5,700	4,000
7	Product D	2,000	3,000	1,000
8	Product E	1,000	2,400	6,000
9	Total net	17,000	16,600	18,000
10	VAT	2,975	2,905	3,150
11	Total gross	19,975	19,505	21,150

Suggest suitable formula for cells:

(a) B9

(b) C10

(c) D11

More advanced spreadsheet techniques (Excel 2010)

Learning outcomes

1.2	**Securely store and retrieve relevant information**
	Students need to be able to:
	• Securely store, backup, archive and retrieve data in line with local policies
	• Rename files in line with local conventions
2.2	**Accurately enter data**
	Students need to know:
	• Why their own data input needs to be accurate
	• Why they may need to select relevant data from different sources and where to paste that data in their spreadsheet
	Students need to be able to:
	• Manually enter data accurately
	• Link data from different sources and across different worksheets
	• Remove duplications in data
	• Import data
3.1	**Select and use a range of appropriate formulas and functions to perform calculations**
	Students need to be able to:
	• Plan, select and use a range of formulas to manipulate and analyse the data
	• Plan, select and use appropriate mathematical and logical functions and statistical techniques

3.2	**Select and use relevant tools to analyse and interpret data**
	Students need to be able to:
	• Assess and select the correct analysis tool for a given task • Analyse data using multiple sorting criteria • Analyse data using multiple filtering criteria • Use Conditional Formatting to enhance decisions • Analyse data using pivot tables and charts • Remove duplicates • Use lookup tables • Select and use appropriate forecasting tools • Summarise data using sub totals
3.4	**Edit and update data**
	Students need to be able to:
	• Change existing data • Include relevant new data in a spreadsheet • Identify and remove any further duplicates • Update relevant new data in a chart
4.1	**Use appropriate tools to identify and resolve errors**
	Students need to be able to:
	• Use formula auditing tools • Select and use error checking tools • Show the formulas within a spreadsheet
4.2	**Assess that new data has been accurately added**
	Students need to be able to:
	• Consider if any new data added to the spreadsheet is included in the analysis • Check new data is fully included in an existing chart
4.3	**Protect integrity of data**
	Students need to know:
	• Why protection of the integrity of their data is important • Why they may need to use and share spreadsheet passwords • With whom they can share spreadsheet passwords
	Students need to be able to:
	• Use data validation to restrict editing • Protect cells and worksheets • Use passwords • Keep data secure from unauthorised use

Assessment context

The advanced techniques covered in this chapter are not covered elsewhere on any other units and you may find some of these techniques completely new to you.

Qualification context

This chapter goes into some detail on the use of passwords to protect access to work and may recall from earlier studies the importance of data protection to maintain confidentiality of sensitive information.

Business context

The more advanced spreadsheet techniques can help management make better business decisions by drilling down through data and applying the various data analysis functions available on spreadsheet software.

Chapter overview

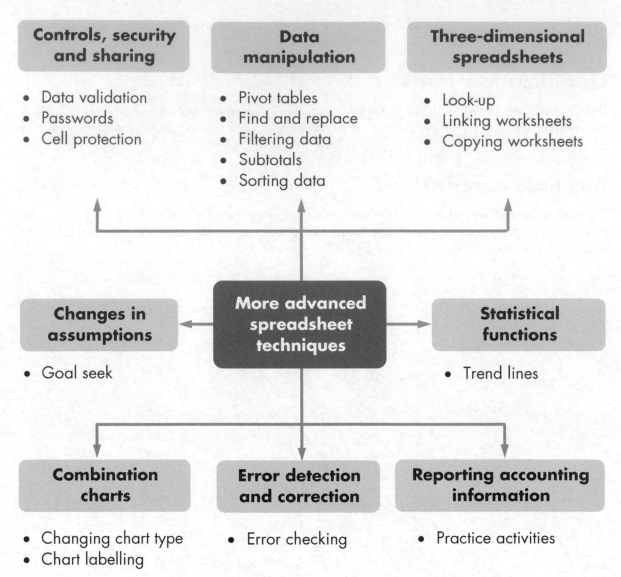

Controls, security and sharing

- Data validation
- Passwords
- Cell protection

Data manipulation

- Pivot tables
- Find and replace
- Filtering data
- Subtotals
- Sorting data

Three-dimensional spreadsheets

- Look-up
- Linking worksheets
- Copying worksheets

Changes in assumptions

- Goal seek

More advanced spreadsheet techniques

Statistical functions

- Trend lines

Combination charts

- Changing chart type
- Chart labelling

Error detection and correction

- Error checking

Reporting accounting information

- Practice activities

Introduction

In this chapter, we build upon the knowledge and skills covered in the preceding introductory chapter and look at advanced spreadsheet techniques, enabling users to manipulate data even further to assist in decision making and reporting.

1 Controls, security and sharing

1.1 Back-ups, passwords and cell protection

There are facilities available in spreadsheet packages which can be used as controls – to prevent unauthorised or accidental amendment or deletion of all or part of a spreadsheet. There are also facilities available for hiding data, and for preventing (or alerting) users about incorrect data.

Saving files and backing up

(a) **Save**. When working on a spreadsheet, save your file regularly, as often as every ten minutes, using **File button>Save** or pressing **Ctrl + S**. This will prevent too much work being lost in the event of a system crash.

Save files in the appropriate **folder** so that they are easy to locate. If you need to save the file to a new folder, choose the '**New folder**' option after clicking **File button>Save**. Where this option is located depends on the operating system you are using. For example, in Windows 7, you simply click the **New folder** button (see below).

Give the folder a suitable name (for example, the name of the client you are working on or following your employer's standard naming practice or other local conventions).

(b) **Save as**. A simple **save** overwrites the existing file. If you use **Save as** then you can give the file a different name, preserving previous versions. For example **Save as** 'Budget Edition 1', 'Budget Edition 2', 'Budget Edition 3'. This is much safer than simply relying on the most recent version – which might be beyond fixing! When saving files it is also possible to save work in other file formats other than spreadsheets. These can include comma-separated values (CSV) and portable document format, more commonly known as pdf.

CSV files are plain text files, but which have markers (commas) which separate (delimit) the fields of data. This can aid conversion to spreadsheets or other applications. They are used when information needs to be exchanged between difference applications. Complex data can be downloaded into the CSV, then opened in a new application.

PDF files are particularly useful when you want the 'look' of a file to be exact. It takes an electronic image of the file, allowing navigation and printing of the file, without the user necessarily having to have the same original software. For example, you may convert an Excel spreadsheet to pdf, allowing the recipient to view the data (even if they do not have Microsoft Excel on their computer).

Assessment focus point

In the assessment it is likely you will need to download a data file, and then **rename** this file as requested in the assessment instructions. Always follow file renaming instructions accurately, and carefully!

(c) **Backups**. Because data – and the computers or storage devices on which it is stored – can easily be lost or destroyed, it is vital to take regular copies or backups. If the data is lost, the backup copy can be used to **restore** the data up to the time the backup was taken. Spreadsheet files should be included in standard backup procedures, for example the daily backup routine.

The backups could be held on a separate external hard drive, or perhaps on a USB memory stick, and should be stored away from the original data, in case there is a fire or other disaster at the organisation's premises. This may be on your hard drive (computer), or on the local network or, increasingly, files can be saved remotely. Businesses are increasingly using 'cloud' (or internet) based storage, such as Amazon, OneDrive (Microsoft), Google, Dropbox etc.

(d) **AutoRecover**. Excel has a built-in feature that saves copies of all open Excel files at a fixed time interval. The files can be restored if Excel closes unexpectedly, such as during a power failure.

Turn on the AutoRecover feature by clicking **File button>Excel Options>Save**.

The default time between saves is every 10 minutes. To change this, click the **Save AutoRecover info every** checkbox and enter any number of minutes between 1 and 120.

In the **AutoRecover file location** box, you can type the path and the folder name of the location in which you want to keep the AutoRecover files.

Protection

(a) **Cell protection/cell locking**. This prevents a user from inadvertently changing cells that should not be changed. There are two ways of specifying which cells should be protected.

(i) All cells are locked except those specifically unlocked.

This method is useful when you want most cells to be locked. When protection is implemented, all cells are locked unless they have previously been excluded from the protection process. You will also see here a similar mechanism for hiding data. In this way specified **ranges** of cells can be locked and unlocked.

Illustration 1: Protecting worksheets

(1) Open the spreadsheet 'Costing Exercise–Finished'.

(2) Highlight the range B2:B5. This contains some of the assumptions on which the cash flow forecast is based and this is the only range of cells that we want to be unlocked and available for alteration.

(3) In the **Home** section of the Ribbon, click on the small arrow beside **Fonts** and then choose **Protection**.

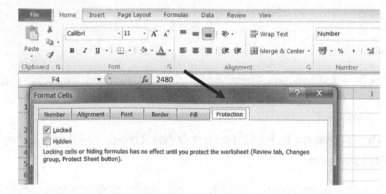

(4) Untick the **Locked** and **Hidden** boxes.

(5) Click on **OK**.

(6) Now go to the **Review** group on the Ribbon.

(7) Click on **Protect Sheet**.

(8) Don't enter a password when prompted, simply click **OK**.

Now investigate what you can change on the spreadsheet. You should find that only cells B2:B5 can be changed. If you try to change anything else a message comes up telling you that the cell is protected.

Click on **Unprotect Sheet** to make every cell accessible to change again.

(ii) Most are unlocked, except those specified as being locked.

This method is useful if only a few cells have to be blocked.

Illustration 1 (continuation): Protecting worksheets

(1) Open the spreadsheet 'Sales discount'.

(2) Assume that we want to lock only the 10,000 in cell C3 and the 5% figure in cell C4.

(3) Select the whole spreadsheet and, as we did above, click on the small arrow beside **Fonts**. Then choose **Protection** and untick the **Locked** and **Hidden** boxes. The cells can still be changed if you do not do this step.

(4) Select the range of cells C3:C4.

(5) In the **Home** section of the Ribbon go to the **Cells** group and click on **Format**.

(6) Click on **Lock Cell**.

(7) Click on **Protect Sheet** from the same **Format** menu. The cells remain editable if you do not do this step.

You are offered the chance to enter a password.

Now you will be prevented from changing just those two cells.

(8) **Hiding and showing formulas** – the same process can be used to hide or show formulas on a worksheet by selecting **Hidden** within **Protection** to hide formulas, and deselect **Hidden** to allow formulas to be seen by users.

(b) **Passwords**. There are two levels of password.

(i) All access to the spreadsheet can be protected and the spreadsheet encrypted. This can be done by:

(1) **File button>Info>Protect Workbook>Encrypt with Password**.

(2) You are then asked to enter and verify a password. Heed the warning: if you forget the password, there's no likelihood of recovery of the spreadsheet.

(3) To remove the password protection use:

File button>Info>Protect Workbook>Encrypt with Password

(4) Then delete the asterisks in the password box and click **OK**.

(ii) The spreadsheet can be password-protected from amendment but can be seen without a password. This can be done as follows:

> (1) At the bottom of the **Save As** dialogue click **Tools**.
>
> (2) Choose **General Options**.
>
> (3) You can choose here again a **Password to open**.
>
> (4) In the **Password to modify** box type a password, then retype it to confirm and click **OK**.
>
> (5) Click **Save**.

Now, if you close the file and re-open it, you will be asked for a password to get full access; without the password you can open it in read-only mode so that it can be seen but not changed.

To keep the integrity of a password system passwords should be kept private and not shared with others. There may sometimes be a need for passwords to be shared between two or more persons. This may be due to a wider access of information that is not of a sensitive nature. If this is the case then organisational policies will need to be adhered to so that access is restricted to those with proper authorisation. An additional level of security may require more frequent changes of passwords when there are multiple users of one password.

1.2 Data validation

Sometimes only a specific type or range of data is valid for a certain cell or cells. For example, if inputting hours worked in a week from a timesheet it could be known that no one should have worked more than 60 hours. It is possible to test data as it is input and to either prevent input completely or simply warn that the input value looks odd. This is known as 'data validation' or 'data restriction'. Errors or warnings can also be shown by circling invalid data in red.

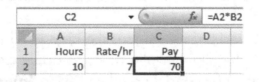

In this simple spreadsheet, C2 holds the only formula; A2 and B2 are cells into which data will be entered, but we want the data to conform to certain rules:

Hours <= 60. If greater than 60, a warning is to be issued.

Rate/hr >=8 and <=20. Data outside that range should be rejected.

Illustration 2: Data validation

(1) Set up a new spreadsheet with the above data and make A2 the active cell. Go to **Data>Data Validation** (in **Data Tools** section).

(2) Under the **Data Validation Settings** tab, **Allow Decimal**, select **less than or equal to** from the drop-down list and enter 60 as the **Maximum**.

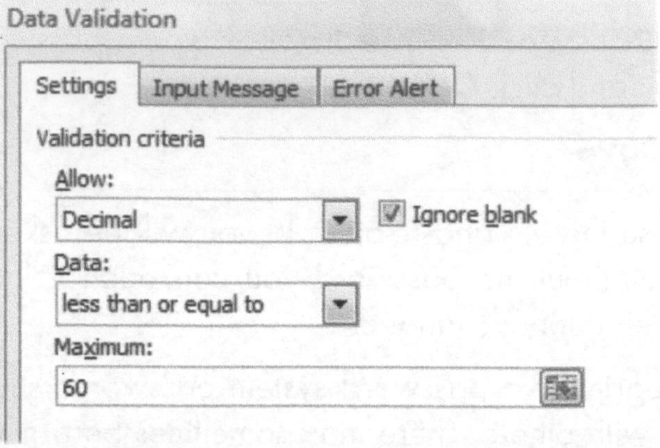

(3) Under the **Input Message** tab enter 'Warning' as the title and 'Hours expected to be less than 60' as the input message.

(4) Under the **Error Alert** tab, change the **Style** to **Warning**, enter 'Attention' as the title and 'Check hours: look too large' as the **Error message**.

(5) Click **OK**.

(6) Now try to enter 70 into A2. You will first see an information message explaining what data is expected, then a warning message and the option to continue.

(7) Now try to set up cell B2 with appropriate messages and to prevent any value outside the range 8–20 from being entered at all.

Assessment focus point

In addition to Error Alerts and Error messages the data validation function can also be used to apply circles to highlight invalid data. To apply circles to your data follow the same routine as above and then select **Circle Invalid Data** from the data validation drop down menu. You need to be aware that these circles can be applied, however, you won't be asked to apply them.

2 Data manipulation

Data manipulation refers to a number of techniques available in Excel for summarising, analysing and presenting data.

Sorting the data

Data can be sorted into ascending or descending numeric order, or alphabetically A-Z or Z-A, from the **Sort & Filter** drop-down menu. A feature here is **Custom Sort** and this allows sorting to be completed on a specified column.

When numeric data has been sorted into groups, Excel can calculate a **subtotal** of each group by selecting **Data>Subtotal**.

Illustration 3: Subtotals

(1) Open a new spreadsheet and enter the following information:

	A	B	C
1	Area	Sales	
2	A	30	
3	A	20	
4	B	90	
5	B	10	
6			

(2) Select cell references A1 to B5.

(3) Select **Data>Subtotals**.

(4) You should see:

Subtotal

At each change in:

Area

Use function:

Sum

Add subtotal to:

☐ Area
☑ Sales

☑ Replace current subtotals
☐ Page break between groups
☑ Summary below data

Remove All   OK   Cancel

Excel will subtotal Areas on the basis of Sales.

(5) Click **OK**.

(6) You should see:

	A	B	C
1	Area	Sales	
2	A	30	
3	A	20	
4	**A Total**	50	
5	B	90	
6	B	10	
7	**B Total**	100	
8	**Grand Total**	150	
9			

Areas A and B have been subtotalled 50 and 100 respectively with an overall Grand Total of 150.

Subtotal formulas

Subtotals can also be calculated using formulas. Popular subtotal formulas include; average, maximum, minimum and a sum of values from a range of data.

Different calculations use an **'operation code'**. An operation code is a specific number inserted within a formula to request Excel to perform a particular operation, for example the number '1' denotes an average calculation. Other operation codes that can be used in a **subtotal** formula include:

Operation	Operation code
1	AVERAGE
4	MAXIMUM
5	MINIMUM
9	SUM

For example, a business has made the following weekly sales units:

	A	B
1		**Sales units**
2	Monday	240
3	Tuesday	300
4	Wednesday	320
5	Thursday	280
6	Friday	300
7	Saturday	440
8	Sunday	360
9		
10	**Average**	
11	**Maximum**	
12	**Minimum**	
13	**Sum**	

The business wishes to calculate the average, maximum, minimum and sum of the range of data using subtotals the following operational codes and formulas can be used:

	A	B
1		**Sales units**
2	Monday	240
3	Tuesday	300
4	Wednesday	320
5	Thursday	280
6	Friday	300
7	Saturday	440
8	Sunday	360
9		
10	**Average**	=SUBTOTAL(1,B2:B8)
11	**Maximum**	=SUBTOTAL(4,B2:B8)
12	**Minimum**	=SUBTOTAL(5,B2:B8)
13	**Sum**	=SUBTOTAL(9,B2:B8)

The calculated values are:

	A	B
1		**Sales units**
2	Monday	240
3	Tuesday	300
4	Wednesday	320
5	Thursday	280
6	Friday	300
7	Saturday	440
8	Sunday	360
9		
10	**Average**	320
11	**Maximum**	440
12	**Minimum**	240
13	**Sum**	2240

Filtering the data

Filtering data allows you to select and display just some of it in the table. This is useful if the table consists of many records, but you only wish to view some of them. Data can be analysed by applying multiple filters, allowing various combinations of data to be analysed.

Illustration 4: Applying a filter to data

(1) Open the 'Stockman Ltd' spreadsheet.

(2) Let's say we just want to find inventory records relating to suppliers B and C.

(3) Select **Filter** from the **Sort & Filter** drop-down menu.

(4) Click on the drop-down arrow that has appeared at the top of the Supplier column.

(5) De-select (ie click on the box to remove the tick) **Select All**, then select B and C.

(6) Click on **OK**.

Only the records relating to suppliers B and C are visible and these can be manipulated (eg sorted) as an independent subset of the whole table.

Note that the other records are still there and are included in the total value figure. It's simply that they have been hidden for presentation.

You will also see a little funnel symbol at the top of the Supplier column; this informs you that there is filtering in place.

Make all the records visible again by removing the filter:

(1) Drop-down arrow in the Supplier column.
(2) Select **Select All**.
(3) Click on **OK**.
(4) Sort the data back into Part code order, if it's not already in that order.

To get rid of the little filter arrows, click on the funnel symbol in the **Sort & Filter** area of the Ribbon to disengage it.

Find and replace

Let's now say that Supplier A Ltd has been taken over and that its name has changed to Acorn plc.

Illustration 5: Using find and replace

(1) Make all the records visible again by removing the filter if you haven't already
(2) Click on the **Find & Select** symbol and select **Find** (or press **Ctrl + F**)
(3) Enter A Ltd in the **Find what**: box
(4) Click on the **Replace** tab and enter Acorn Plc in the **Replace with**: box
(5) Click on **Replace All**

Note. You could instead click on **Find & Select>Replace** (or press **Ctrl + H**) as a shortcut.

You should see that all occurrences of 'A Ltd' have been replaced by 'Acorn plc'.

If no range is specified before this step then the whole spreadsheet would be affected. If a range is specified, the search and replace occurs only within that range.

Concatenate

The concatenate function is used to combine two text cells into a single cell.

This is done by using the formula = CONCATENATE(text1, [text 2]...)

C1		⁃	⋮	×	✓	f_x	=CONCATENATE(A1,B1)		
	A	B	C	D	E	F	G	H	
1	Spread	sheet	Spreadsheet						
2									
3									

If the formula is used as shown above, the words will be joined together with no space inbetween.

If a space is to be included between the words, this can be achieved by using quotation marks around a single space between the two text references in the formula.

=CONCATENATE(text1, " ",[text 2]...)

	A	B	C	D	E	F	G	H
				fx	=CONCATENATE(C1," ",D1)			
1	Spread	sheet	Spreadsheet	skills	Spreadsheet skills			
2								
3								
4								

This is particularly useful when joining data such as first name and last name.

Removing duplicates

If you wish to remove duplicate data from a worksheet this can be achieved by selecting the required data, then **Data>Remove Duplicates**. From here you can choose the columns to show the number of duplicate and unique data contained. This technique will help ensure that data has been entered accurately.

2.1 Pivot tables

Pivot tables are a very powerful way of analysing data. Look at the following simple example relating to sales by a music company.

	A	B	C
	Pivot table example		
1	**Sales data**		
2			
3	**Customer**	**Source**	**Amount spent (£)**
4	Bill	CDs	50
5	Chris	Vinyl	10
6	Sandra	Merchandise	30
7	Graham	CDs	45
8	Chris	Merchandise	20
9	Chris	Vinyl	10
10	Chris	CDs	10
11	Caroline	Merchandise	30
12	Graham	Tickets	75
13	Fred	Vinyl	30
14	Bill	CDs	20
15	Graham	CDs	60
16	Chris	Vinyl	10
17	Sandra	Tickets	50
18	Bill	Tickets	26
19	Caroline	Vinyl	24
20			
21		Total	£500

The information has simply been listed and totalled on the spreadsheet. It would be useful to be able to show:

- Sales per customer
- Sales by source

Ideally, we would like to produce a table which displays sales by both source and by customer: this type of table is called a pivot table.

Illustration 6: Creating a pivot table

(1) Open the spreadsheet file called 'Pivot Table Example' which contains the above data.

(2) Select the range A4:C19.

(3) On the Ribbon, select **Insert>PivotTable**.

(4) Select the **Existing Worksheet** radio button on the **Create PivotTable** option window.

(5) Enter E4 as the location.

(6) Click **OK**. The **PivotTable Field List** window opens.

(7) Check Customer, Source, Amount spent (£).

(8) You will see that Customer and Source go by default into **Row Labels**. The resulting table is quite useful, but not quite what we wanted.

Therefore:

(9) Drag Customer from **Row Labels** to **Column Labels**.

The pivot table is now transformed into the two-dimensional table we want.

(10) Tidy it up a little by selecting F5 to L5 and right-justifying these names by clicking on the appropriate **Home>Alignment** button on the Ribbon.

Note the two drop-down arrows on the pivot table that allow filtering of the data.

Sum of Amount spent (£)	Column Labels ▾						
Row Labels ▾	Bill	Caroline	Chris	Fred	Graham	Sandra	Grand Total
CDs	70		10		105		185
Merchandise		30	20			30	80
Tickets	26				75	50	151
Vinyl		24	30	30			84
Grand Total	96	54	60	30	180	80	500

If you had difficulty with this, the spreadsheet called 'Pivot Table Result Excel 2010' is available within the downloaded files.

Experiment with different settings. Clicking on the pivot table will bring up the **PivotTable Field List** window again, if it has disappeared.

Note that if the original data is altered, the pivot table does **not** change until you right-click on it and select **Refresh** from the list of options.

Pivot charts

The information contained in a pivot table can be visually presented using a pivot chart.

(1) Click on any cell inside the pivot table.

(2) On the **Insert** tab, click **Pivot chart** and select one of the graph types. For example, 'clustered column'

> **Note.** Any changes you make to the pivot table will be immediately reflected in the pivot chart, and vice versa.

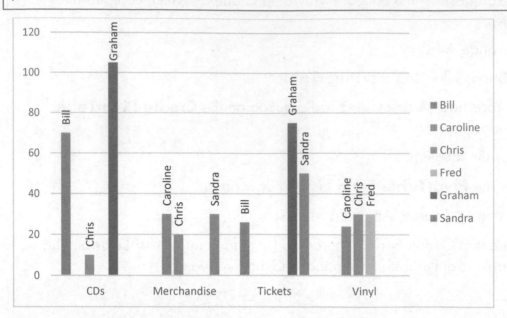

2.2 Sharing workbooks

It is possible to share a workbook with colleagues, so that the same file can be viewed by more than one person at a time. This can be done in a number of ways.

Send as an attachment

One way to share a spreadsheet with colleagues is to send it as an attachment in an email. If your computer is set up with a mail client such as Microsoft Outlook you can click **File Button>Save & Send>Send Using Email** to quickly send the spreadsheet you are working on as an attachment.

Alternatively, you can first draft the email and attach the spreadsheet using your email program's options and the Windows Explorer menu.

However, if each recipient of the email makes changes to the document, this will lead to the existence of a number of different versions of the same document, and a potential loss of version control. This is not, therefore, a recommended method of sharing spreadsheets.

Save to a shared network server

Another way to make a spreadsheet available to colleagues is to save it in a place on the network server that is also accessible to them. Anyone with access to that particular location will be able to open the file; if more than one person tries to open the file, only the first person will be able to make changes to it. Anyone else subsequently opening the file will only be able to open a 'Read Only' version of it: they will be able to view the contents, but not make any changes.

This method prevents loss of version control but is not particularly useful if other people wish to make changes at the same time.

Share workbook method

A more practical method is to use the inbuilt sharing function in Excel. This allows different people to open and make changes to the same document at the same time, and for these changes to be tracked.

Click the **Review** tab on the Ribbon. In the **Changes** section, click the **Share Workbook** button. Click the **Editing** tab and select **Allow changes by more than one user at the same time**. From this tab you can also see who has the document open.

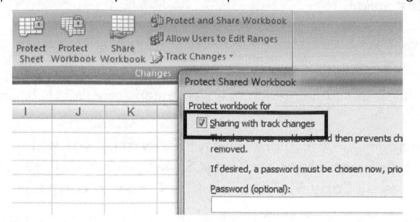

Other settings are available from the **Advanced** tab, such as choosing how long to keep the change history for, how frequently to update changes and what to do if users make conflicting changes.

To stop any tracked changes from being lost, click **Protect and Share Workbook** and click **Sharing with tracked changes**. This option also allows you to set a password so only those with the password can make changes.

3 Three-dimensional (multi-sheet) spreadsheets

3.1 Background

In early spreadsheet packages, a spreadsheet file consisted of a single worksheet. As mentioned earlier, Excel provides the option of multi-sheet spreadsheets, consisting of a series of related sheets.

For example, suppose you were producing a profit forecast for two regions, and a combined forecast for the total of the regions. This situation would be suited to using separate worksheets for each region and another for the total. This approach is sometimes referred to as working in **three dimensions**, as you are able to flip between different sheets stacked in front of, or behind, each other. Cells in one

sheet may **refer** to cells in another sheet. So, in our example, the formulas in the cells in the total sheet would refer to the cells in the other sheets.

Excel has a series of 'tabs', one for each worksheet, at the bottom of the spreadsheet.

3.2 How many worksheets?

Excel can be set up so that it always opens a fresh file with a certain number of worksheets ready and waiting for you. Click on **Office button>Excel Options>Popular**, and set the number **'Include this many sheets'** option to the number you would like each new workbook to contain (sheets may be added or deleted later).

If you subsequently want to insert more sheets you just click on the new sheet tab.

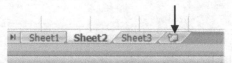

By default, sheets are called Sheet 1, Sheet 2 etc. However, these may be changed. To rename a sheet in Excel, right-click on its index tab and choose the **Rename** option. You can drag the sheets into different orders by clicking on the tab, holding down the mouse button and dragging a sheet to its new position. Index tabs can also be formatted in a variety of colours by right-click on its index tab and selecting the **Tab Color** option.

3.3 Pasting from one sheet to another

When building a spreadsheet that will contain a number of worksheets with identical structure, users often set up one sheet, then copy that sheet and amend its contents.

To copy a worksheet in Excel, from within the worksheet you wish to copy, select **Home>Cells>Format>Move or Copy Sheet** (or right-click the worksheet tab and select **Move or Copy Sheet**) and tick the **Create a copy** box.

A 'Total' sheet would use the same structure, but would contain formulas totalling the individual sheets.

Illustration 7: Linking worksheets

The following illustration shows how to link worksheets with formulas.

Formulas on one sheet may refer to data held on another sheet. The links within such a formula may be established using the following steps.

Step 1   In the cell that you want to refer to a cell from another sheet, type =.

Step 2   Click on the index tab for the sheet containing the cell you want to refer to, and select the cell in question.

Step 3   Press **Enter**.

---

(1) Open the spreadsheet called '3D spreadsheet example'.

This consists of three worksheets. The Branch A and Branch B sheets hold simple trading accounts and income statements. There are both numbers and formulas in those sheets. The Company sheet contains only headings, but is set out in the same pattern as the two branch sheets.

We want to combine the Branch figures onto the Company sheet.

(2) On the Company sheet, make D2 the active cell.

(3) Enter **=**

(4) Click on Branch A and click on D2.

(5) Enter **+**

(6) Click on Branch B and click on D2.

(7) Press **Enter**.

You will see that the formula ='Branch A'!D2+'Branch B'!D2 is now in cell D2 of the Company sheet and that the number displayed is 500,000, the sum of the sales in each branch.

In the Company sheet, copy D2 (**Ctrl+C**) and then paste (**Ctrl+V**) to D3, D4, C6, C7, D8, and D9 to complete the income statement.

The company sheet will now look like this:

	A	B	C	D
	3D spreadsheet example [Compatibility Mode]			
1	**Company**		£	£
2	Revenue			500,000
3	Cost of sales			270,000
4	Gross profit			230,000
5	Expenses:			
6	Selling and distribution		70,000	
7	Administration		45,000	
8				115,000
9	Net profit			115,000
10				
11				

This is arithmetically correct, but needs lines to format it correctly.

Use the border facility in **Home>Font** to insert appropriate single and double lines (**borders**) in the cells:

The final consolidated results should look like:

Note that if you change any figures in Branch A or Branch B, the figures will also change on the Company spreadsheet.

Files and documents (eg spreadsheets and Word documents) can also be **direct referenced** and linked by using **Paste Special>Paste Link**. To check the status of any links created go to **Data>Edit Links** and this will show a list of links their source and options to update and break links.

3.4 Uses for multi-sheet spreadsheets

There are a wide range of situations suited to the multi-sheet approach. A variety of possible uses follow.

(a) A spreadsheet could use one sheet for variables, a second for calculations and a third for outputs.

(b) To enable quick and easy **consolidation** of similar sets of data, for example the financial results of two subsidiaries or the budgets of two departments.

(c) To provide different views of the same data. For instance, you could have one sheet of data sorted into product code order and another sorted into product name order.

3.5 Formatting data as a table

You can format data within a spreadsheet as a table. This provides you with another way to present and manipulate data.

Creating a table

First we will create a table and then we'll look at what we can do with it.

Illustration 8: Formatting a table

(1) **Open** the 'Tables example' spreadsheet from the downloaded files. This uses almost the same data as in the previous exercise, so it should look familiar to you.

(2) Select the cells that contain the data (A3 to G15).

(3) On the **Home** tab of the Ribbon, select **Format as Table** from the **Styles** section.

(4) A gallery of styles will appear, so choose one of the formats (any one will do). Check that the correct data for the table is selected in the white box and tick the box **My table has headers**.

(5) Click **OK**.

(6) Your table should now look something like this, depending on which format you chose:

	A	B	C	D	E	F	G
1	Stockman Ltd						
2							
3	Part cod	Supplie	Quantit	Reorder leve	Unit pric	Value	Order neede
4	129394	A Ltd	124	100	20	2,480.00	
5	129395	B Ltd	4325	4500	14	60,550.00	Yes
6	129396	F Ltd	4626	4000	12	55,512.00	
7	129397	A Ltd	583	500	14	8,162.00	
8	129398	D Ltd	43	50	37	1,591.00	Yes
9	129399	E Ltd	837	1000	65	54,405.00	Yes
10	129400	B Ltd	84	50	34	2,856.00	
11	129401	F Ltd	4847	5000	20	96,940.00	Yes
12	129402	D Ltd	4632	4000	10	46,320.00	
13	129403	A Ltd	41	40	34	1,394.00	
14	129404	E Ltd	5578	5000	25	139,450.00	
15	129405	C Ltd	5	10	35	175.00	Yes

You will notice that there are **Sort & Filter** drop-down arrows at the top of each column in the header row. This is just one of the benefits of formatting data as a table: automatic **Sort & Filter**.

Other benefits of formatting data as a table

Other benefits include:

(a) **Easy row and column selection**

Move the cursor to the top of the header row of the table and it will change to a thick pointing arrow. When you click, just the data in that column will be selected (and not the empty cells below the data). You can select data rows in a similar way.

The whole table can be selected by hovering near the table's top-left corner until the arrow becomes thick and starts pointing towards the bottom right-hand corner.

(b) **Visible header row when scrolling**

When you scroll down past the bottom of the table, the column letters become the table's column names so long as you have clicked anywhere inside the table before starting scrolling.

	Part code	Supplier	Quantity	Reorder level	Unit price	Value	Order needed
4	129394	A Ltd	124	100	20	2,480.00	
5	129395	B Ltd	4325	4500	14	60,550.00	Yes
6	129396	F Ltd	4626	4000	12	55,512.00	
7	129397	A Ltd	583	500	14	8,162.00	
8	129398	D Ltd	43	50	37	1,591.00	Yes
9	129399	E Ltd	837	1000	65	54,405.00	Yes
10	129400	B Ltd	84	50	34	2,856.00	
11	129401	F Ltd	4847	5000	20	96,940.00	Yes
12	129402	D Ltd	4632	4000	10	46,320.00	
13	129403	A Ltd	41	40	34	1,394.00	
14	129404	E Ltd	5578	5000	25	139,450.00	
15	129405	C Ltd	5	10	35	175.00	Yes
16							

(c) **Automatic table expansion**

Type anything into any of the cells around the table and the table will automatically grow to include your new data. The formatting of the table will automatically adjust (this will also happen if you insert or delete a row or column).

(d) **Automatic formula copying**

If you enter a formula in a cell around the table and click **Enter**, the column will automatically resize to fit the formula, which is automatically copied down to fill the entire column alongside your data.

Changing the design of the table

You can change how the table looks by clicking anywhere in the table and selecting **Design** tab from the **Table Tools** toolbar.

Table Tools

Design

ns

Table Style

From here there are a number of **Table Style Options** that you can play around with, such as formatting a **First Column** or **Last Column**, adding a **Total Row** and changing the **Table Style**.

You can also choose to give your table a name, so that any formula you enter which uses the figures from the table will refer to that table by its name.

So, for example, type 'Parts' into the **Table Name** box:

Table Name:

Parts

Resize Table

Now any formula entered in the column next to the table will refer to the table by name. Try it!

	Font		Alignment		Number		Styles		Cells	

=Parts[[#This Row],[Quantity]]*Parts[[#This Row],[Unit price]]

C	D	E	F	G	H	I	J	K	L	M

antit	Reorder leve	Unit pric	Value	Order neede						
		£	£							
124	100	20	2,480.00							
4325	4500	14	60,550.00	Yes	=Parts[[#This Row],[Quantity]]*Parts[[#This Row],[Unit price]]					
4626	4000	12	55,512.00							
583	500	14	8,162.00							
43	50	37	1,591.00	Yes						
837	1000	65	54,405.00	Yes						

Table tools

From the **Design** tab you can also:

- Choose to **Remove Duplicates**, which, as the name suggests, removes duplicate data from the table.

- Remove the table formatting completely, by selecting **Convert to Range**. You may then wish to clear the formatting. You can easily do this by clicking **Clear** on the **Editing** section of the **Home** tab and choosing **Clear Formats**.

Σ AutoSum
Fill
Clear
Sort & Find &
Filter Select

Clear All
Clear Formats
Clear Contents
Clear Comments

3.6 Look-up tables

The Look-up function allows you to find and use data that is held in a table.

VLOOKUP is used for finding data in **v**ertical columns.

HLOOKUP is used for finding data in **h**orizontal rows.

Here is a simple example:

	A	B	C	D	E	F	G	H	I
1	**Salesman Ltd**								
2	Part code	VATcode	Unit price		VAT rate	20.0%			
3			£						
4	129394	1	20.00						
5	129395	1	14.00		Invoice				
6	129396	0	12.00						
7	129397	0	14.00						
8	129398	1	37.00		Part code	Quantity	Unit price	VAT	£
9	129399	0	65.00		129396	10	12.00	0	120.00
10	129400	1	34.00					Net	120.00
11	129401	0	20.00					VAT	0.00
12	129402	1	10.00					Total	120.00
13	129403	0	34.00						
14	129404	0	25.00						
15	129405	1	35.00						
16									
17									

On the left is a price list. If a part has a VAT code of 1, then VAT will be charged at the rate as set in cell F2; if the VAT code is 0, then no VAT is chargeable.

To create this invoice, you would look down the part numbers column until you found 129396. You would then read across to find the unit price and VAT code and, together with the quantity sold, you could create the invoice.

This process has been automated in the spreadsheet 'Salesman Ltd'.

---

(1) Open the spreadsheet called 'Salesman Ltd'.
(2) Click on cell G9 to reveal the use of the VLOOKUP function.

Cell G9 holds the formula = VLOOKUP(E9,A4:C15,3, FALSE)

This means: look for the value held in cell E9, in the first row of the range A4:C15, and return the value in the third column of the range; it will return the price relating to the part number. FALSE (at the end of the statement) asks it to find an exact match so if a non-existent part code is entered in E9 you will get an error message (**#N/A**).

Similarly, cell H9 holds the formula = VLOOKUP(E9,A4:C15,2) and will return the VAT code relating to the part number.

Cell I11 holds a conditional (IF) function that will calculate VAT if the VAT code is 1 and insert 0 if the VAT code is 0.

Note that some cells have been formatted to show two decimal places and some to show no decimal places. Cell F2 is formatted as a percentage and, because VAT might need to be changed, VAT is held in only one location with other cells referring to it.

Try out different part codes and quantities in the invoice.

3.7 Importing data to Excel

You may wish to include data in a spreadsheet from, say, a Microsoft Word document, a PowerPoint presentation or another spreadsheet.

The easiest way to do this is select the text you wish to include, click the **Home** tab and click **Copy** (or press **Ctrl + C**).

Open the spreadsheet that you wish to use the data in (if it is not already open) and click the **Paste** button (or press **Ctrl + V**).

> **Assessment focus point**
>
> Ensure you understand, and can practice using, the main data manipulation tools in this section. Practising using the different data tools will build understanding of what information is produced and any limitations.

4 Changes in assumptions (what-if? analysis)

In Chapter 1 we referred to the need to design a spreadsheet so that **changes in assumptions** do **not** require **major changes** to the spreadsheet. In our 'Costing exercise' workbook we set up two separate areas of the spreadsheet, one for assumptions and opening balances and one for the calculations and results. We could simply change the values in the assumptions cells to see how any changes in assumptions affect the results.

However, if we have more than one value to change, or we want to see the result of a number of different assumption changes, we can use one of the three 'What-if' functions.

4.1 Data tables

A **data table** is a way to see different results by altering an input cell in a formula. You can create one- or two-variable data tables.

Let's try creating a one-variable data table.

---

(1) Open the spreadsheet called 'Mortgage'.

(2) Enter 1% to 10% in cells E8 to N8 as shown below.

	A	B	C	D	E	F	G	H	I	J	K	L	M	N
1	Assumptions													
2														
3	Annual interest rate		10%											
4	Amount of loan (£)		20,000											
5	Period of loan		20											
6														
7	Calculation of monthly repayments over a reducing balance mortgage lasting (years)													
8					1%	2%	3%	4%	5%	6%	7%	8%	9%	10%
9	Monthly repayment			-£193.00										
10														

(3) Select cells D8 to N9.

(4) **Click Data>What-If Analysis>Data Table**.

(5) Here you want your data table to fill in the values in row 9, based on the results if the value in cell C3 were to change to a different percentage, so choose the **Row input cell** box and enter C3.

You should get the following results:

	1%	2%	3%	4%	5%	6%	7%	8%	9%	10%
-£193.00	-91.9789	-101.177	-110.92	-121.196	-131.991	-143.286	-155.06	-167.288	-179.945	-193.004

The table would look better if the numbers were formatted in the same way as the first result in cell D9. An easy way to copy a format from one cell to another is to click on the cell whose format you wish to copy, then click the **Format Painter** button on the **Clipboard** area of the **Home** tab, and then click on the cells you wish to format.

Try it now. Click on cell D9, then click the **Format Painter** button. Now select cells E9:N9. You should see:

	1%	2%	3%	4%	5%	6%	7%	8%	9%	10%
-£193.00	-£91.98	-£101.18	-£110.92	-£121.20	-£131.99	-£143.29	-£155.06	-£167.29	-£179.95	-£193.00

Note. If you double-click the **Format Painter** button you can then click any number of cells afterwards to apply that same format. To deactivate the **Format Painter**, simply click **Esc** (Escape).

Now let's try a two-variable data table using the same workbook. This time we want to see the result if both the interest rate and the number of years of the loan change.

(1) Rename the worksheet you have been working on to 'One variable'. Now select Sheet2 (or insert a new worksheet if necessary) and rename it 'Two variable'. This is the sheet that we will now use.

(2) **Copy** the data on the 'One variable' worksheet (**Ctrl + C**) and paste (**Ctrl + V**) into the new worksheet.

(3) Select cells E8 to N8 and move them down by one cell (ie to E9 to N9). You can do this by hovering over the selected cells until a cross with four arrow heads appears, then click and drag to cell E9. Alternatively, **Cut (Ctrl + X)** and then **Paste (Ctrl + V)** to cell E9.

(4) In cells D10 to D14, insert different loan periods. We have used 10, 15, 20, 25 and 30 years as shown below:

-£193.00	1%	2%	3%	4%	5%	6%	7%	8%	9%	10%
10										
15										
20										
25										
30										

(5) Select cells D9 to N14.

(6) Click **Data>What-If Analysis>Data Table**.

(7) Here you want the data table to fill in the values based on the results if the value in cell C3 were to change to a different percentage (as shown in row 9) and also if the loan period in C5 changes (as shown in column D). So, choose the **Row input cell** box and enter C3 and then select the **Column input cell** box and enter C5.

You should get the following results:

-£193.00	1%	2%	3%	4%	5%	6%	7%	8%	9%	10%
10	-£175.21	-£184.03	-£193.12	-£202.49	-£212.13	-£222.04	-£232.22	-£242.66	-£253.35	-£264.30
15	-£119.70	-£128.70	-£138.12	-£147.94	-£158.16	-£168.77	-£179.77	-£191.13	-£202.85	-£214.92
20	-£91.98	-£101.18	-£110.92	-£121.20	-£131.99	-£143.29	-£155.06	-£167.29	-£179.95	-£193.00
25	-£75.37	-£84.77	-£94.84	-£105.57	-£116.92	-£128.86	-£141.36	-£154.36	-£167.84	-£181.74
30	-£64.33	-£73.92	-£84.32	-£95.48	-£107.36	-£119.91	-£133.06	-£146.75	-£160.92	-£175.51

Format cells E10 to N14 in the same way as cell D9.

Finally, practise saving the file as 'Mortgage – Data tables' in a new folder on your computer using **File button>Save as**. Choose an appropriate name for the folder – it's your choice!

4.2 Scenarios

The **Scenarios** function allows you to change information in cells that affect the final totals of a formula and to prepare instant reports showing the results of all scenarios together.

Using the spreadsheet 'Costing Exercise – Finished', we will show the result of changing the following assumptions:

(a) The chargeout rate for the Accounting Technician is now £30.00.

(b) The cost of a laptop has increased to £115.00 per week.

(c) The increase in chargeout rate for the secretary has been altered to 8%.

You could simply change the relevant cells in the spreadsheet to reflect these changes in assumptions. However, we are going to use the Scenario Manager function.

Illustration 9: Using the scenarios function

(1) Select the **Data** tab and from the **Data Tools** section click **What-If Analysis>Scenario Manager**.

(2) Click **Add** and give the scenario an appropriate name, for example 'Original costing exercise'.

(3) Press the tab button or click in the **Changing cells** box and, based on the information we used above, select the cells with the changing data, ignoring the change to the opening bank balance. To select cells that are not next to each other, use the **Ctrl** button. You should **Ctrl-click** on cells B4, B6, B7.

(4) Click **OK**.

(5) You are now asked for **Scenario Values**. This will show the values currently in the cells specified, which are our original figures, so click **OK**.

Scenario Values

Enter values for each of the changing cells.

1:	$B$4	21.45
2:	$B$6	100
3:	$B$7	0.1

Add   OK   Cancel

(6) We now need to enter our new values. Click **Add** and type a new **Name** (for example 'Costing exercise 2'). The **Changing Cells** box will already contain the correct cells.

(7) Click **OK**.

(8) In the **Scenario Values** boxes change the values as follows and click **OK**.

Scenario Values

Enter values for each of the changing cells.

1:	$B$4	30.00
2:	$B$6	115
3:	$B$7	0.08

Add   OK   Cancel

(9) Your second scenario should be highlighted. Now if you click on **Show**, the figures in your assumptions table should automatically change and you can view the results.

L22 f_x

	A	B	C	D	E	F	G
1	**Internal chargeout rates**						
2	Divisional chief accountant	£72.50					
3	Assistant accountant	£38.00					
4	Accounting technician	£30.00					
5	Secretary	£17.30					
6	Laptop cost	£115.00					
7	Chargeout rate	8%					
8							
9	**Costs**	*Week 1*	*Week 2*	*Week 3*	*Week 4*	*Total*	
10	Divisional chief accountant	£0.00	£326.25	£489.38	£435.00	£1,250.63	
11	Assistant accountant	£760.00	£1,520.00	£1,330.00	£0.00	£3,610.00	
12	Accounting technician	£960.00	£1,200.00	£1,125.00	£0.00	£3,285.00	
13	Secretary	£259.50	£557.93	£695.98	£0.00	£1,513.40	
14	Laptops	£230.00	£230.00	£230.00		£690.00	
15	**Total**	**£1,979.50**	**£3,604.18**	**£3,640.35**	**£435.00**	**£10,349.03**	
16							
17	**Hours**	Week 1	Week 2	Week 3	Week 4	Total	
18	Divisional chief accountant		4.5	6.75	6	17.25	
19	Assistant accountant	20	40	35		95	
20	Accounting technician	32	40	37.5		109.5	
21	Secretary	15	32.25	37.25		84.5	
22	Total	**67**	**116.75**	**116.5**	**6**	**300.25**	
23							
24	Laptops	2	2	2			
25							
26							
27							

(10) Click back on your original 'Costing exercise' and then click **Show** and the numbers will change back.

Note. You may need to make your screen smaller to view the whole sheet at the same time. You can do this by clicking **View** on the Ribbon and then, in the **Zoom** section, clicking on **Zoom** and choosing a smaller percentage. 75% should be perfect.

You can also easily and quickly create a report from the scenarios.

(1) Click **Data>What-If Analysis>Scenario Manager**.

(2) Click the **Summary** button.

(3) In the **Result** cells box choose the cells to go into the report, ie the ones you want to see the results of. As we are interested in the final cost, select cell F15. This creates a separate Scenario Summary worksheet. Open the 'Costing Exercise – What-if' spreadsheet if you do not see the following report.

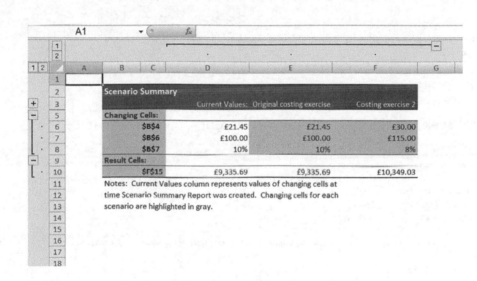

4.3 Goal seek

What if you already know the result you want from a formula but not the value the formula itself needs to calculate the result? In this case you should use the **Goal Seek** function, which is located in the **Data Tools** section of the **Data** tab on the Ribbon.

Open the original 'Mortgage spreadsheet' from the downloaded files. Let's assume that we have enough income to pay a monthly mortgage payment of £300 and want to know how many years it will take to pay off the mortgage.

(1) Copy the data on Sheet 1 and paste it to Sheet 2.

(2) Click **Data>What-If Analysis>Goal Seek**.

(3) **Set cell** to $D$9, as this is the figure we know and enter -300 in the **To value** box (make sure that you enter a negative figure to match the figure already in D9).

(4) Enter $C$5 in the **By changing cell** box, as this is the figure we are looking for.

(5) Click **OK**.

	A	B	C	D	E	F	G	H	I	J
1	Assumptions									
2										
3	Annual interest rate		10%							
4	Amount of loan (£)		20,000							
5	Period of loan		20	years						
6										
7	Calculation of monthly repayments over a reducing balance mortgage lasting (years)									20
8										
9	Monthly repayment		-£193.00							
10										
11										
12										
13										
14										
15										
16										
17										

Goal Seek

Set cell: $D$9
To value: -300
By changing cell: $C$5

OK   Cancel

Goal seek will find the solution, 8.14 years, and insert it in cell C5.

	A	B	C	D	E	F	G	H	I	J
1	Assumptions									
2										
3	Annual interest rate		10%							
4	Amount of loan (£)		20,000							
5	Period of loan		8.143044	years						
6										
7	Calculation of monthly repayments over a reducing balance mortgage lasting (years)									8.143044
8										
9	Monthly repayment		-£300.00							
10										
11										
12										
13										
14										
15										
16										
17										

Goal Seek Status

Goal Seeking with Cell D9 found a solution.

Target value: -300
Current value: -£300.00

Step
Pause

OK   Cancel

Assessment focus point

In the exam, you may be asked to use one or more of these forecasting tools, such as **Goal Seek**. It is essential that you have a full understanding of what each tool may be used for and how it can answer the exam question. Read the question carefully to ensure the tool you select answers the question in the most appropriate manner.

5 Statistical functions

Assessment focus point

It is unlikely that you will be tested on statistical functions such as preparing trends, moving averages and histograms. The following information is provided to develop your spreadsheet skills further in these areas. If you wish, you may skip section 5 and move directly to section 6.

5.1 Linear regression, trends and forecasts

Excel contains powerful statistical tools for the analysis of information, such as how costs vary with production volumes and how sales vary through the year.

Look at the following example of costs and volume:

Month	Volume Units	Costs £
1	1,000	8,500
2	1,200	9,600
3	1,800	14,000
4	900	7,000
5	2,000	16,000
6	400	5,000

It is clear that at higher production volumes costs are higher, but it would be useful to find a relationship between these variables so that we could predict what costs might be if production were forecast at, say, 1,500 units.

The first investigation we could perform is simply to draw a graph of costs against volume. Volume is the independent variable (it causes the costs) so should run on the horizontal (x) axis.

Illustration 10: Trend lines

Open the spreadsheet called 'Cost_volume' and draw a scatter graph showing cost against volume, with appropriate labels and legends.

(1) Select the range B1:C7.

(2) Using **Insert/Charts** from the Ribbon, choose the top left Scatter graph type).

It should look something like the following:

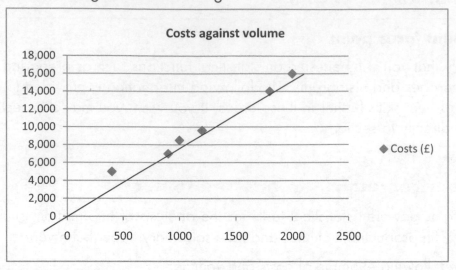

The straight line through the points has been manually drawn here to show that there's clearly a good association between volume and cost, because the points do not miss the line by much; but we want to analyse this properly so that we can make a fairly good prediction of costs at output of, say 1,500 units.

Lines of the sort above have a general equation of the type:

y	=	**mx + b**
Here **y**	=	Total costs
x	=	Volume
m	=	Variable cost per unit (the slope of the line)
b	=	The fixed cost (where the line crosses the y axis: the cost even at zero volume)

Excel provides two easy ways of finding the figures we need for predicting values.

Find the trend:

(1) On the same spreadsheet (Cost_volume), enter 1,500 in cell B9.

(2) Now click on cell C9.

(3) From the Ribbon choose **Formulas>More Functions>Statistical**.

(4) Scroll down the list until you get to **TREND** and choose that.

(5) For **Known_y's** select the range C2:C7.

(6) For **Known_x's** select the range B2:B7.

(These ranges are the raw material which the calculation uses)

For **New_x's**, enter B9, the volume for which we want the costs to be predicted.

The number 12,003 should appear in cell C9. That is the predicted cost for output of 1,500 units – in line with the graph. In practice, we would use 12,000. Altering the value in B9 will produce the corresponding predicted cost.

A second way of analysing this data will allow us to find the variable and fixed costs of the units (**m** and **b** in the equation **y = mx +b**).

(1) To find **m** use the statistical function **LINEST** and assign the **Known_y's** and **Known_x's** as before. You should get the answer 7.01, the variable cost per unit.

(2) To find the intersection, **b**, use the statistical function **INTERCEPT**. You should get the answer 1,486.

Note. These can be used to predict the costs of 1,500 units by saying:

Total costs = 1,486 + 7.01 × 1,500 = 12,001, more or less as before.

The spreadsheet called 'Cost_volume finished' contains the graph, and the three statistical functions just described.

5.2 Moving averages

AAT only require knowledge of the area of moving averages, but it is important to understand what we mean by moving averages and how they can be calculated. Note that you will not be asked to reproduce this in the live assessment, however, you need to understand what it is and how it works.

Look at this data

Year	Quarter	Time series	Sales £000
20X6	1	1	989.0
	2	2	990.0
	3	3	994.0
	4	4	1,015.0
20X7	1	5	1,030.0
	2	6	1,042.5
	3	7	1,036.0
	4	8	1,056.5

Year	Quarter	Time series	Sales £000
20X8	1	9	1,071.0
	2	10	1,083.5
	3	11	1,079.5
	4	12	1,099.5
20X9	1	13	1,115.5
	2	14	1,127.5
	3	15	1,123.5
	4	16	1,135.0
20Y0	1	17	1,140.0

You might be able to see that the data follows a seasonal pattern: for example there always seems to be a dip in Quarter 3 and a peak in Quarter 2. It is more obvious if plotted as a time series of sales against the consecutively numbered quarters.

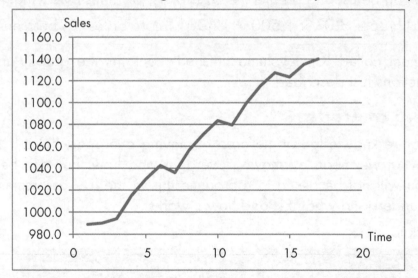

The **moving average** technique attempts to even out the seasonal variations. Here, because we seem to have data repeating every four readings, a four-part moving average would be appropriate. If you were trading five days a week and wanted to even out the sales, a five-part moving average would be suitable.

The moving average is calculated as follows:

Take the first four figures and average them:

$$\frac{(989.0 + 990.0 + 994.0 + 1,015.0)}{4} = 997.0$$

Then move on one season:

$$\frac{(990.0 + 994.0 + 1,015.0 + 1,030.0)}{4} = 1,007.3$$

... and so on, always averaging out all four seasons. Each average will include a high season and a low season.

That's rather tedious to do manually and Excel provides a function to do it automatically. To access this analysis function you must have the **Excel Analysis ToolPak** installed. If it is installed there will be an **Analysis>Data Analysis** tab in the **Data** section of the Ribbon.

If it is not already installed, you can install it as follows:

(1) Click the **File Button**, and then click **Excel Options**.

(2) Click **Add-Ins**, and then from the **Manage** box, select **Excel Add-Ins**.

(3) Click **Go**.

(4) In the **Add-Ins available** box, select the **Analysis ToolPak** checkbox, and then click OK.

Tip. If **Analysis ToolPak** is not listed in the **Add-Ins available** box, click **Browse** to locate it.

If you are prompted that the **Analysis ToolPak** is not currently installed on your computer, click **Yes** to install it. This may take a little time, so be patient!

(1) Open the spreadsheet called 'Time series'.
(2) Select **Data>Data analysis>Moving average**.
(3) Select D2:D18 as the **Input Range**.
(4) Enter 4 as the **Interval** (a four-part moving average).
(5) Enter F2 as the **Output Range**.
(6) Check **Chart Output**.
(7) Click on **OK**.

Don't worry about the error messages – the first three simply mean that you can't do a four-part average until you have four readings.

Move your cursor onto the moving average figures and move it down, one cell at a time, to see how the averages move.

Notice on the graph how the Forecast line (the moving average) is much smoother than the Actual figures. This makes predicting future sales much easier.

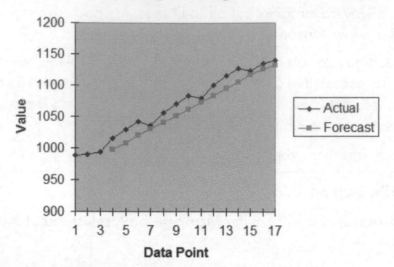

Moving average

5.3 Mean, mode and median

These are three measures of what is known as the 'location' of data – they give an indication of whereabouts the data is clustered.

Mean (or arithmetic mean) is the ordinary average (add up the readings and divide by the number of readings).

Mode is the most frequently occurring item. For example, in a shoe shop, the arithmetic mean of shoe sizes is not much use. The shopkeeper is more interested in the most common shoe size.

Median is the value of the middle item if they are arranged in ascending or descending sequence. As well as medians you can have 'quartiles' (upper and lower) dividing the population into the top one-quarter, lowest three-quarters (or *vice versa*) and 'deciles' (10:90 splits).

Excel allows all of these measures to be calculated (or identified) easily.

---

(1) Open the spreadsheet called 'Student Results'.

This lists the exam results of 23 students. They are currently displayed in alphabetical order. Don't worry about the column headed 'Bins' for now.

Enter 'Mean' in cell A28, then make cell B28 active.

(2) Choose **Formulas>Σ AutoSum>Average** and accept the range offered. 58.56 is the arithmetic mean of the marks.

(3) Enter 'Median' in cell A29, then make cell B29 active.

(4) Choose **Formulas>More Functions>Statistical>MEDIAN**.

(5) Enter the range B4:B26 for Number 1.

You should see 57 as the median.

Check this by sorting the data into descending order by score, then counting up to the 12th student, Kate. (She's the middle student and scored 57.)

(6) Enter 'Percentile' in cell A30, 0.75 in cell C30 and then make cell B30 active.

(7) Choose **Formulas>More Functions>Statistical>PERCENTILE.EXC.**

(8) Enter the range B4:B26 and C30 as the K value.

The reported value is 68, the figure which divides the top quarter from the bottom three-quarters of students.

(9) Enter 'Mode' in cell A31, then make cell B31 active.

(10) Choose **Formulas>More Functions>Statistical>Mode**.

(11) Enter the range B4:B26.

The reported value is 65 (that occurs more frequently than any other score).

5.4 Histograms

AAT only require knowledge of histograms, and what their uses are in business. Note that you will not be asked to reproduce these in the live assessment, however, you need to understand what they are and how they work.

A **histogram** is a graph which shows the frequency with which certain values occur. Usually the values are grouped so that one could produce a histogram showing how many people were 160–165cm tall, how many >165–170, >170–175 and so on.

Excel can produce histogram analyses provided the **Analysis ToolPak** is installed. Installation was described earlier in the section about time series.

To demonstrate the histogram we will use the Student results spreadsheet again.

Illustration 11: Histogram preparation

(1) Open the 'Student results' spreadsheet if it is not already open.

You will see that in E5 to E13 is a column called 'Bins'. This describes the groupings that we want our results to be included in, so here we are going up the result in groups (bins) of ten percentage points at a time; the histogram will show how many results are in 0–10, 11–20, 21–30 etc.

(2) Choose **Data>Data Analysis>Histogram**.

(3) Enter the range B4:B26 as the **Input Range**.

(4) Enter E5:E13 as the **Bin Range**.

(5) Choose **New Worksheet Ply** and enter 'Histogram analysis' in the white text box.

(6) Tick **Chart Output**.

(7) Click on **OK**.

The new worksheet will show the data grouped into the 'bins' by frequency and also shows a histogram.

The spreadsheet 'Student results finished' shows the finished spreadsheet complete with histogram in the Histogram analysis worksheet.

6 Combination charts

Excel allows you to combine two different charts into one. For example you may wish to compare sales to profits. This is also known as showing two graphs on one axis.

To do this we create a chart from our data as before.

Illustration 12: Combination charts

(1) Open the 'Combination chart' spreadsheet from the downloaded files. This provides data for the number of sales of precious metal in 2009 and 2010. The price at which the precious metal is sold per kilo goes up and down according to the market.

(2) Select the data that will go into your chart (cells A1 to C9)

(3) Click **Insert** and then choose your chart type. For this example let's choose a **2-D clustered column** chart. The chart doesn't really help us to understand the relationship between the two different sets of data.

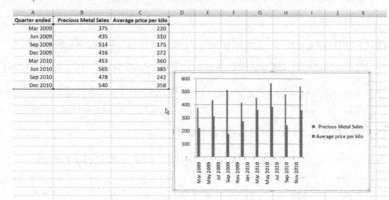

(4) A more visual way of displaying the average price data might be to see it in a line set against the number of sales. So click on any Average price column, right-click and select **Change Series Chart Type**.

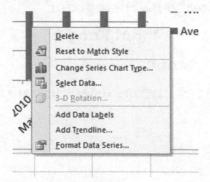

(5) Select **Line with Markers** and click **OK**. The chart will look like this:

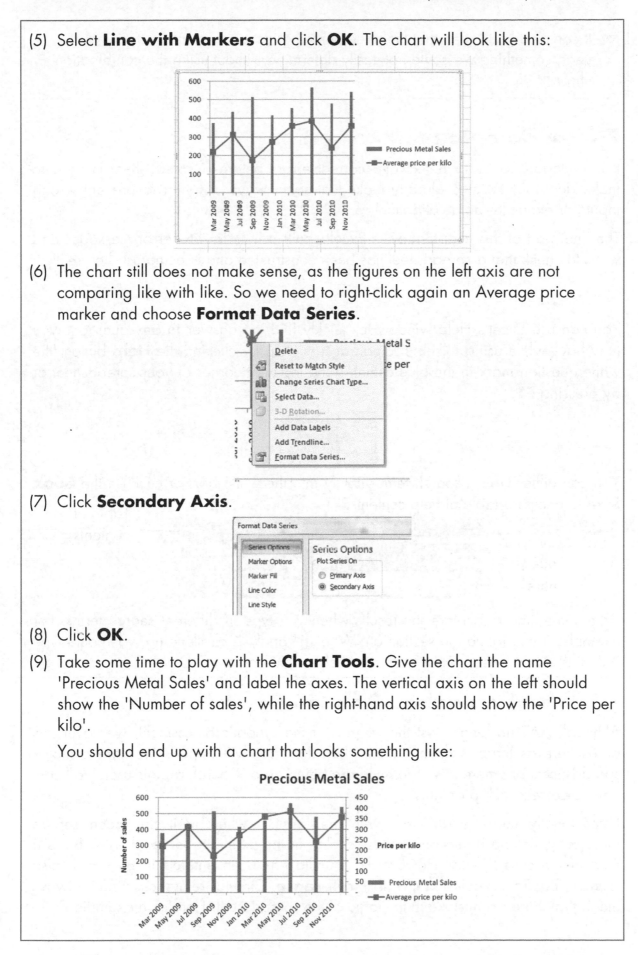

(6) The chart still does not make sense, as the figures on the left axis are not comparing like with like. So we need to right-click again an Average price marker and choose **Format Data Series**.

(7) Click **Secondary Axis**.

(8) Click **OK**.

(9) Take some time to play with the **Chart Tools**. Give the chart the name 'Precious Metal Sales' and label the axes. The vertical axis on the left should show the 'Number of sales', while the right-hand axis should show the 'Price per kilo'.

You should end up with a chart that looks something like:

It can clearly be seen that the price per kilo dips in the third quarter of each year, something we could not easily determine without using the combination chart.

7 Error detection and correction

It is important to try to detect and correct errors before a spreadsheet is used to make decisions. We've already looked at some ways of trying to prevent wrong input (for example, data validation).

The final part of this chapter covers Excel's built-in help facility, error messages and ways to check that a spreadsheet has been constructed and is being used correctly.

7.1 Help

You can use Excel's Help window to quickly find the answer to any questions you may have while using Excel. You can access Help by clicking the **Help** button (the white question mark in the blue circle) in the top-right corner of your spreadsheet or by pressing **F1**.

You can either type a search term directly into the white bar, or click on the **book icon** to access a table of help contents.

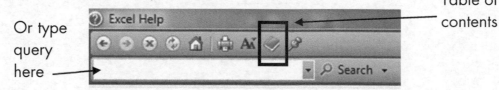

Take some time to explore the results when you type in different search terms. For example, if you found the section on 'What-If?' analysis challenging, you could type 'What if' into the search bar to receive help on this topic.

7.2 Removing circular references

Although AAT no longer test this as part of the synoptic assessment, we cover this areas here as there is often a time when the error will appear on more complex spreadsheets or where lots of formula are being used. Therefore, it is useful to know how to correct such problems.

Occasionally there is an issue with the formula whereby it has been set up incorrectly, linking it into an 'endless circle'. In the example below, the cell B5 is a total of the cells B3–B4. However, a formula has been entered in B4 which also refers to B5. This is called a **circular reference**. Circular references nearly always mean that there's a mistake in the logic of the spreadsheet. Here's an example:

	A	B
1		
2		£
3	Basic salary	20,000
4	Bonus 10% of total pay	=0.1*B5
5	Total pay	20,000

A warning will be displayed by Excel:

Microsoft Excel

Circular Reference Warning

One or more formulas contain a circular reference and may not calculate correctly. Circular references are any references within a formula that depend upon the results of that same formula. For example, a cell that refers to its own value or a cell that refers to another cell which depends on the original cell's value both contain circular references.

For more information about understanding, finding, and removing circular references, click OK. If you want to create a circular reference, click Cancel to continue.

OK   Cancel

In our example, it is relatively easy to find the cause of the problem, but in a large spreadsheet it can be difficult. Clicking **OK** will provide help and will bring up a help screen referring you to **Formulas>Formula Auditing>Circular References** on the Ribbon.

Trace Precedents   Show Formulas
Trace Dependents   Error Checking
Remove Arrows

Error Checking...

Trace Error

Circular References   √ $B$5
                           $B$4

7.3 Using trace precedents

Tracing precedents and dependents

As spreadsheets are developed it can become difficult to be sure where figures come from and go to (despite being able to display formulas in all the cells). A useful technique is to make use of the 'trace precedents' and 'trace dependents' options. These are available on the **Formulas** section of the Ribbon.

Illustration 13: Auditing formulas

(1) Open the 'Precedent example' spreadsheet from the downloaded files and make cell F4 active.

(2) Choose the **Formulas** section of the Ribbon and click on **Trace Precedents** in the **Formula Auditing** group of icons.

You should see:

	A	B	C	D	E	F
1	BUDGETED SALES FIGURES					
2		Jan	Feb	Mar		Total
3		£'000	£'000	£'000		£'000
4	North	2,431	3,001	2,189		7,621
5	South	6,532	5,826	6,124		18,482
6	West	895	432	596		1,923
7	Total	9,858	9,259	8,909		28,026

BPP LEARNING MEDIA

Now it is very obvious that anything in column E, like April figures, will not be included in the total.

(3) Click on **Remove Arrows** in the **Formula Auditing** group.

(4) Make B4 the active cell.

(5) Click on **Trace Dependents**. This will show what cells make use of this cell:

	A	B	C	D	E	F
1	BUDGETED SALES FIGURES					
2		Jan	Feb	Mar		Total
3		£'000	£'000	£'000		£'000
4	North	2,431	3,001	2,189		7,621
5	South	6,532	5,826	6,124		18,482
6	West	895	432	596		1,923
7	Total	9,858	9,259	8,909		28,026

Assessment focus point

Although AAT have stated that it is unlikely that you will be tested on the ability to trace precedents and dependents, it is a valuable skill in being able to check your spreadsheet for any potential problems, and useful in auditing formulas (which is a skill tested by the AAT).

7.4 Rounding errors

The ability to display numbers in a variety of formats (eg to no decimal places) can result in a situation whereby totals that are correct may actually look incorrect.

Illustration 14: Rounding errors

The following illustration shows how apparent rounding errors can arise.

	A	B	C
1	Petty cash		
2	Week ending 31/12/20X6		
3			£
4	Opening balance		231.34
5	Receipts		32.99
6	Payments		-104.67
7	Closing balance		159.66

	A	B	C
1	Petty cash		
2	Week ending 31/12/20X6		
3			£
4	Opening balance		231
5	Receipts		33
6	Payments		-105
7	Closing balance		160

Cell C7 contains the formula =SUM(C4:C6). The spreadsheet on the left shows the correct total to two decimal places. The spreadsheet on the right seems to be saying that 231 + 33 – 105 is equal to 160, which is not true: it's 159 (check it). The **reason for the discrepancy** is that both spreadsheets actually contain the values shown in the spreadsheet on the **left**.

However, the spreadsheet on the right has been formatted to display numbers with **no decimal places**. So, individual numbers display as the nearest whole number, although the actual value held by the spreadsheet and used in calculations includes the decimals.

The round function

One solution, that will prevent the appearance of apparent errors, is to use the **ROUND function**. The ROUND function has the following structure: ROUND (value, places). 'Value' is the value to be rounded. 'Places' is the number of places to which the value is to be rounded.

The difference between using the ROUND function and formatting a value to a number of decimal places is that using the ROUND function actually **changes** the **value**, while formatting only changes the **appearance** of the value.

In the example above, the ROUND function could be used as follows. The following formulas could be inserted in cells D4 to D7.

D4 = ROUND(C4,0)
D5 = ROUND(C5,0)
D6 = ROUND(C6,0)
D7 = Round (SUM(D4:D6),0)

Column C could then be hidden by highlighting the whole column (clicking on the C at the top of the column), then right clicking anywhere on the column and selecting **Hide**. Try this for yourself, hands-on using the 'Rounding example' spreadsheet.

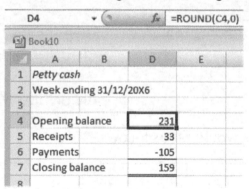

Note that using the ROUND function to eliminate decimals results in slightly inaccurate calculation totals (in our example 160 is actually 'more correct' than the 159 obtained using ROUND). For this reason, some people prefer not to use the function, and to make users of the spreadsheet aware that small apparent differences are due to rounding.

Roundup and Rounddown

The ROUND function can be adapted to round numbers to a required number of decimal places, either by rounding up, rounding down.

Roundup

For example, if a cost per unit was £100.828392 and management wished to express this value rounded up to 0, 1, and 2 decimal places then the following **Roundup** formulas could be used.

	A	B	C
1	Costs	Rounding required	Roundup
2	100.828392	0	=ROUNDUP(A2,B2)
3	100.828392	1	=ROUNDUP(A3,B3)
4	100.828392	2	=ROUNDUP(A4,B4)

Looking at the formula shown in cell C2 the A2 reference picks up the value to be rounded, and B2 is the number of decimal places to round up to. In C2 we are requesting Excel to round the value up to zero places, and so on.

The rounded up results would then be as follows.

	A	B	C
1	Costs	Rounding required	Roundup
2	£100.828392	0	£101.00
3	£100.828392	1	£100.90
4	£100.828392	2	£100.83

Using the same value £100.828392 and using the Rounddown formula, the formulas would be.

	A	B	C
1	Costs	Rounding required	Rounddown
2	100.828392	0	=ROUNDDOWN(A2,B2)
3	100.828392	1	=ROUNDDOWN(A3,B3)
4	100.828392	2	=ROUNDDOWN(A4,B4)

The rounded down results would be as follows.

	A	B	C
1	Costs	Rounding required	Rounddown
2	£100.828392	0	£100.00
3	£100.828392	1	£100.80
4	£100.828392	2	£100.82

7.5 Identifying error values

Error checking can be turned on by **File button>Excel options>Formulas** and checking **Enable background error checking**. There is a list that allows you to decide which errors are to be highlighted. If a green triangle appears in a cell, then the cell contains an error.

Other information about the nature of the error will also be supplied:

#########	The column is not wide enough to hold the number. Widen the column or choose another format in which to display the number (no green triangle here as it is not a 'real' error – just a presentation problem).
#DIV/0!	Commonly caused by a formula attempting to divide a number by zero (perhaps because the divisor cell is blank).
#VALUE!	Occurs when a mathematical formula refers to a cell containing text; eg if cell A2 contains text, the formula =A1+A2+A3 will return #VALUE!. Functions that operate on ranges (eg SUM) will not result in a #VALUE! error as they ignore text values.
#NAME?	The formula contains text that is not a valid cell address, range name or function name. Check the spelling of any functions used (eg by looking through functions under Formulas>Insert Function).
#REF!	The formula includes an invalid cell reference, for example a reference to cells that have subsequently been deleted. If you notice the reference immediately after a deletion, use Ctrl+Z to reverse the deletion.
#NUM!	This error is caused by invalid numeric values being supplied to a worksheet formula or function. For example, using a negative number with the SQRT (square root) function. To investigate, check the formula and function logic and syntax. The Formula Auditing toolbar may help this process (see below).
#N/A	A value is not available to a function or formula; for example omitting a required argument from a spreadsheet function. Again, the Formula Auditing toolbar may help the investigation process (see below).

7.6 Tracing and correcting errors

If you do see one of the above errors you can trace where it came from by clicking on the cell with the error; then, from the **Formulas** tab of the Ribbon, choose **Formula Auditing** and click the down arrow next to **Error Checking**. Lines will appear pointing to the data that has produced the error.

If you simply click the **Error Checking** button, it will automatically check the current worksheet and alert you to any errors.

Finally, you can click **Evaluate Formula** to be taken step by step through it so that you can identify the error.

BPP
LEARNING MEDIA

8 Reporting accounting information

You will be able to use a variety of tools and have developed your skills in using spreadsheets to analyse and present data. In the exam it is vital that you answer the question, following closely any instructions regarding presentation and data to be analysed. Sometimes the question may specify the type of presentation (table, graph, chart) sometimes the examiner will ask you to use your own judgement on how to best present the information.

You may be tested on your ability to be able to differentiate between what information is required and what will not aid you answering the question.

Practice using the spreadsheet tools using the illustrations, examples and test your learning questions provided. Ensure that you can organise, analyse and present the data in the most efficient and appropriate manner.

The ten **practice activities** at the end of this book will give valuable practice in making judgments on how to apply functions and formulas in specific situations to obtain the required output.

Chapter summary

- It is important to save and **backup your work regularly**. You can use **Save as** to give various versions of the same document different names.

- It is important to **control the security** of spreadsheets through passwords, locking (protecting) cells against unauthorised or accidental changes, or data validation on input.

- Spreadsheet packages permit the user to work with **multiple sheets** that refer to each other. This is sometimes referred to as a three-dimensional spreadsheet.

- Excel offers sophisticated data handling including **filtering**, **pivot tables** and **look-up tables**.

- **Combination charts** allow you to show two sets of data on one axis of your chart.

- **Goal seek** is a function that allows you to explore various results using different sets of values in one or more formulas.

- **Error detection** and prevention is important in spreadsheet design and testing. There are useful facilities available, such as tracing precedents and dependents, identification of circular references and error reports, as well as Excel's built-in help function.

- It is important to make judgements on how to apply functions and formulas when using spreadsheet software when **reporting accounting information**.

- **Backup:** Where a copy file is taken so work can be restored if original work is lost or destroyed

- **Cell locking:** A data protection method that prevents users from changing the content of locked cells

- **Circular references:** Situations where a cell contains a formula and the same cell reference is itself in the formula cell

- **Data table:** A table that allows data results to change based on changing assumptions

- **Data validation:** A function that can provide warning messages and other protection when invalid data is entered

- **Find and replace:** Method of locating specific data in a worksheet and replacing with alternative data if required

- **Formula auditing:** An error-checking approach that shows the connections between formulas and cells

- **Goal seek:** Function that can identify the inputs required into a formula to arrive at a known outcome

- **Histogram:** A graph which shows the frequency with which certain values occur

- **Look-up tables:** A function that allows users to find and use data held in a table

- **Mean:** An average value calculated by adding up values and dividing by the number of values

- **Median:** The value that is the middle value when values are arranged in an ascending or descending sequence

- **Mode:** The most frequently occurring value within a sequence of values

- **Moving average:** A technique that evens out any seasonal variations so that trends can be more easily identified

- **Passwords:** A data protection system that restricts user access by a unique sequence of characters

- **Pivot table:** A table that allows users to change its structure by selecting and choosing the style of how data is presented

- **Save:** The process of 'saving' the contents of a file so that any work completed is retained. The action of saving will overwrite the existing file

- **Save as:** Similar to save but the file being 'saved as' is given a different name

- **Scenarios:** A function that allows users to change information to discover how changes can alter the outcome of a scenario

- **Sort and filter:** A function that allows data to be sorted in a requested order, for example A-Z. A filter allows users to select and display part of the contents of a table of data

- **Trace precedents and dependents:** Error-detection methods that use tracer arrows to identify data used in formulas and relationships between active cells

Test your learning

1 What command is used to save a file under a different name?

2 What part of the Ribbon do you go to set up checking procedures on the input of data?

3 List three possible uses for a multi-sheet (3D) spreadsheet.

4 What does filtering do?

5 What is a trend line?

6 What is the median?

7 What is a histogram?

8 What does the error message #DIV/0! mean?

Introduction to spreadsheets (Excel 2013)

Learning outcomes

1.1	**Organise data in a timely manner** Students need to be able to: • Identify all customer requirements, including deadlines • Consider the use of a template or design a bespoke spreadsheet • Plan and design the spreadsheet to meet customer needs • Develop a spreadsheet for specific accountancy purposes
2.1	**Select relevant data** Students need to know: • When they have sufficient data and information Students need to be able to: • Select valid, reliable and accurate data • Select relevant raw data from different sources • Differentiate between what information is required and what information is not required
2.3	**Format data** Students need to be able to: • Use a range of appropriate formatting tools to aid understanding and present the data effectively
3.1	**Select and use a range of appropriate formulas and functions to perform calculations** Students need to be able to: • Plan, select and use a range of formulas to manipulate and analyse the data • Plan, select and use appropriate mathematical and logical functions and statistical techniques to perform calculations

3.3	**Select and use appropriate tools to generate and format charts**
	Students need to be able to:
	• Critically select and use a range of charts to summarise and present information
	• Develop and format charts appropriately to aid understanding
	– Altering scales
	– Altering formatting axes
	– Labelling charts
	– Change data series colour and/or format
	• Produce an output in a format suitable to ensure equality of opportunity
5.1	**Prepare reports**
	Students need to be able to:
	• Insert headers and footers
	• Hide rows and or columns
	• Format columns, rows and outputs to enhance understanding of the relevant data
	• Adjust margins, orientation and print area
	• Produce a summary sheet linking to other data and/or worksheets
5.2	**Report accounting information**
	Students need to know:
	• Why it is important to confirm that the result meets customer requirements
	Students need to be able to:
	• Ensure that data produced is suitable for publication, using the appropriate house style
	• Show all worksheet formulas in a format suitable for publication
	• Communicate the completed information to the customer appropriately

Assessment context

The *Spreadsheets for Accounting* unit is assessed as part of the Level 3 *Advanced Diploma in Accounting* Unit Assessment. You will be requested to present your answers in an appropriate spreadsheet format to show a whole range of skills and knowledge.

Qualification context

Specific spreadsheet software use only appears on the *Spreadsheets for Accounting* unit, however some of the concepts used, for example saving files, use of passwords and accurate input of data, may be familiar to you either from use of spreadsheets or from experience using other software packages.

Business context

The use of spreadsheet packages are a vital part of business life. Spreadsheets are known for their speed and accuracy in calculations and also their data manipulation capabilities. This means that spreadsheets are indispensable in the work of accountants and other finance professionals.

Chapter overview

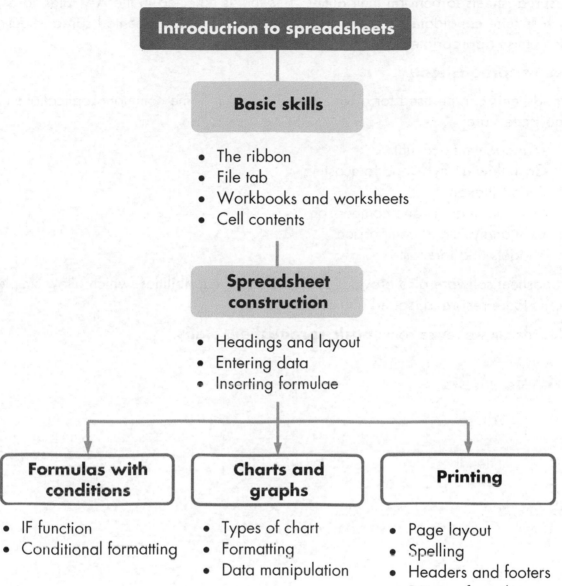

Introduction to spreadsheets

Basic skills

- The ribbon
- File tab
- Workbooks and worksheets
- Cell contents

Spreadsheet construction

- Headings and layout
- Entering data
- Inserting formulae

Formulas with conditions

- IF function
- Conditional formatting

Charts and graphs

- Types of chart
- Formatting
- Data manipulation

Printing

- Page layout
- Spelling
- Headers and footers
- Printing formulas
- Annotating output

Introduction

The vast majority of people who work in an accounting environment are required to use spreadsheets to perform their duties. This fact is reflected in the AAT Standards, which require candidates to be able to produce clear, well-presented spreadsheets, which utilise appropriate spreadsheet functions and formulas.

Uses of spreadsheets

Spreadsheets can be used for a wide range of tasks. Some common applications of spreadsheets are:

- Management accounts
- Cash flow analysis and forecasting
- Reconciliations
- Revenue analysis and comparison
- Cost analysis and comparison
- Budgets and forecasts

Spreadsheet software also provides basic database capabilities, which allow simple records to be recorded, sorted and searched.

In this section we revise some **basic spreadsheet skills**.

1 Basic skills

1.1 The Ribbon

1.2 File tab

The **File tab** is a menu tab and provides access to several options.

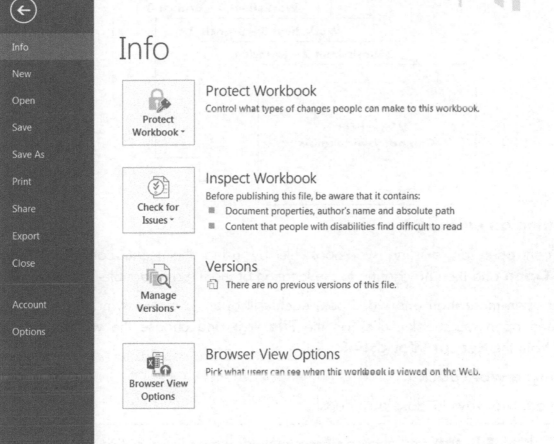

1.3 Workbooks and worksheets

At the bottom-left of the spreadsheet window you will see tabs which are known as **Worksheets**:

When **New** is selected from **File tab**, you will be given an option to choose from a number of templates. Choose **Blank workbook** to create a new blank **workbook**. The workbook consists of one or more **worksheets**. Think of worksheets as **pages** that make up the workbook. By default, a new Excel workbook starts out with three worksheets, although this can be changed (see later).

Worksheets can provide a convenient way of organising information. For example, consider a business consisting of three branches. Worksheets 2 – 4 could hold budget information separately for each branch. When entering formulas into cells it is possible to refer to cells in other worksheets within the workbook so it would then be possible for Worksheet 1 to act as a **summary sheet** linking the totals of the budget information for the whole business. Effectively, a 'three-dimensional' structure can be set up. We look at this in more detail later.

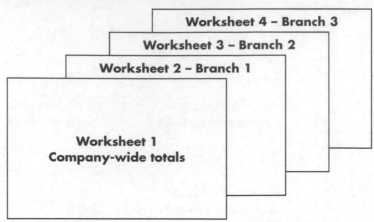

Opening an existing workbook

You can open an existing workbook file by using the menu commands **File tab>Open** and then navigating to the location of the file and double-clicking on it.

If you open more than one workbook, each will open in a new window. To swap between open workbooks, click on the **File tab** and choose the workbook you want from the **Recent Workbooks** list.

Closing a workbook

There are two ways to close a spreadsheet file:

(1) Click the **File tab** and choose **Close** (ninth down on list of options), or

(2) Click on the '**x**' in the top right-hand corner of the window.

In both cases, if you have made any changes to the spreadsheet you will be asked if you want to save them. Choose **Save** to save any changes (this will overwrite the existing file), **Don't Save** to close the file without saving any changes, or **Cancel** to return to the spreadsheet.

1.4 Cell contents

The contents of any cell can be one of the following:

(a) **Text.** A text cell usually contains **words**. Numbers that do not represent numeric values for calculation purposes (eg a Part Number) may be entered in a way that tells Excel to treat the cell contents as text. To do this, enter an apostrophe before the number: '451, for example.

(b) **Values.** A value is a **number** that can be used in a calculation.

(c)   **Formulas.** A formula **refers to other cells** in the spreadsheet, and performs some type of computation with them. For example, if cell C1 contains the formula =A1 − B1, cell C1 will display the result of the calculation, subtracting the contents of cell B1 from the contents of cell A1. In Excel, a formula always begins with an equals sign: = . This alerts the program that what follows is a formula and not text or a value. There is a wide range of formulas and functions available.

Illustration 1: Cell contents

Open the workbook called 'ExcelExample1'. This is one of the files available for download from https://learningmedia.bpp.com/catalog?pagename=AAT_Spreadsheets.

You can open a file by using the menu commands:

File tab>Open

then navigating to and double-clicking on the file called 'ExcelExample1'.

Note. Throughout this Course Book we want spreadsheets to recalculate every time a figure is changed. This is the normal or default setting, so it is likely your spreadsheets already do this. But, if they don't, then:

(1) Click the **File tab**, click **Options**, and then click the **Formulas** category.

(2) To recalculate all dependent formulas every time you make a change to a value, formula or name, in the **Calculation options** section, under **Workbook Calculation**, click **Automatic**. This is the default calculation setting.

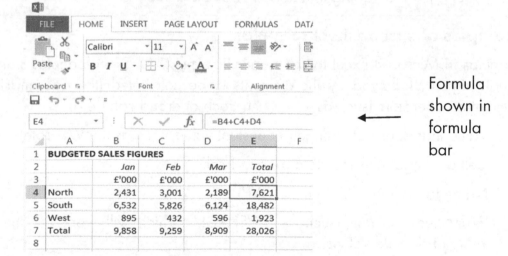

Formula shown in formula bar

You should see the worksheet illustrated above. Click on cell E4.

Look at the formula bar.

Note. If the formula bar is not visible, choose the **View** tab and check the **Formula Bar** box.

Note the important difference between:

(1)   What is shown in cell E4: 7,621.

(2)   What is actually in cell E4: this is shown in the formula bar and it tells us that cell E4 is the result of adding together the contents of cells B4, C4 and D4.

The formula bar allows you to see and edit the contents of the active cell. The bar also shows, on the left side, the cell address of the active cell (E4 in the illustration above).

Select different cells to be the active cell, by using the up/down/right/left arrows on your keyboard or by clicking directly on the cell you want to be active. Look at what is in the cell and what is shown in the formula bar.

The **F5** key is useful for moving around within large spreadsheets. If you press the function key **F5**, a **Go To** dialogue box will allow you to specify the cell address you would like to move to. Try this out.

Also experiment by holding down **Ctrl** and pressing each of the direction arrow keys in turn to see where you end up. Try using the **Page Up** and **Page Down** keys and also try **Home** and **End** and **Ctrl** + these keys. Try **Tab** and **Shift/Tab**, too. These are all useful shortcuts for moving quickly from one place to another in a large spreadsheet.

When dealing with large worksheets it can be useful to **Freeze** rows or columns so that specified ranges of data (eg headings) remain 'frozen' while scrolling and navigating throughout a worksheet. To do this select the data you wish frozen and select your choice by going to **View>Freeze Panes**.

Examples of spreadsheet formulas

Formulas in Microsoft Excel follow a specific syntax. All Excel formulas start with the equals sign =, followed by the elements to be calculated (the operands) and the calculation operators (such as +, -, /, *). Each operand can be a:

*   Value that does not change (a constant value, such as the VAT rate)

*   Cell or range reference to a range of cells

*   Name (a named cell, such as 'VAT')

*   Worksheet function (such as 'AVERAGE', which will work out the average value of defined values)

Formulas can be used to perform a variety of calculations. Here are some examples:

(a)   =C4*5. This formula **multiplies** the value in C4 by 5. The result will appear in the cell holding the formula.

(b)   =C4*B10. This **multiplies** the value in C4 by the value in B10.

(c)   =C4/E5. This **divides** the value in C4 by the value in E5. (* means multiply and / means divide by.)

(d)   =C4*B10–D1. This **multiplies** the value in C4 by that in B10 and then **subtracts** (or minus) the value in D1 from the result. Note that generally Excel will perform multiplication and division before addition or subtraction. If in any doubt, use brackets (parentheses): =(C4*B10)–D1.

(e)   =C4*120%. This **adds** 20% to the value in C4. It could be used to calculate a price including 20% VAT.

(f)   =(C4+C5+C6)/3. Note that the **brackets** mean Excel would perform the addition first. Without the brackets, Excel would first divide the value in C6 by 3 and then add the result to the total of the values in C4 and C5.

(g)   = 2^2 gives you 2 **to the power** of 2, in other words 2 squared. Likewise = 2^3 gives you 2 cubed, and so on.

(h)   = 4^(1/2) gives you the **square root** of 4. Likewise 27^(1/3) gives you the cube root of 27, and so on.

Displaying spreadsheet formulas

It is sometimes useful to see all formulas held in your spreadsheet to enable you to see how the spreadsheet works. There are two ways of making Excel **display the formulas** held in a spreadsheet.

(a)   You can 'toggle' between the two types of display by pressing **Ctrl** +` (the latter is the key above the **Tab** key). Press **Ctrl** +` again to go back to the previous display.

(b)   You can also select the **File tab>Options>Advanced>Display options for this worksheet** and tick **Show formulas in cells instead of their calculated results**.

The formulas for the spreadsheet we viewed earlier are shown below.

	A	B	C	D	E
1	BUDGETED S/				
2		Jan	Feb	Mar	Total
3		£'000	£'000	£'000	£'000
4	North	2431	3001	2189	=B4+C4+D4
5	South	6532	5826	6124	=B5+C5+D5
6	West	895	432	596	=B6+C6+D6
7	Total	=B4+B5+B6	=C4+C5+C6	=D4+D5+D6	=E4+E5+E6
8					
9					
10					
11					

The importance of formulas

Look carefully at the example above and note which cells have formulas in them. It is important to realise that:

- If a cell contains a value, such as sales for North in January, then that data is entered as a number

- If a cell shows the result of a calculation based on values in other cells, such as the total sales for January, then that cell contains a formula

This is vital, because now if North's January sales were changed to, say, 2,500, the total would be automatically updated to show 9,927. Also the total for North would change to 7,690.

Try that out by clicking on cell B4 to make it active, then typing 2,500, followed by the **Enter** key. You should see both the totals change.

Now re-enter the original figure of 2,431 into cell B4.

Similarly, if a number is used more than once, for example a tax rate, it will be much better if the number is input to one cell only. Any other calculations making use of that value should refer to that cell. That way, if the tax rate changes, you only have to change it in one place in the spreadsheet (where it was originally entered) and any calculations making use of it will automatically change.

Your first function

In the example above, totals were calculated using a formula such as:

=+B4+C4+D4

That is fine provided there are not too many items to be included in the total. Imagine the difficulty if you had to find the total of 52 weeks for a year. Adding up rows or columns is made much easier by using the **SUM** function. Instead of the formula above, we could place the following calculation in cell E4:

= SUM (B4:D4)

This produces the sum of all the cells in the range B4 to D4. Now it is much easier to add up a very long row of figures (for example, SUM(F5:T5)) or a very long column of figures (for example, SUM(B10:B60)).

There are three ways in which the SUM function can be entered. One way is simply to type =SUM(B4:D4) when E4 is the active cell. However, there is a more visual and perhaps more accurate way.

Make E4 the active cell by moving the cursor to it, using the arrow keys or by clicking on it.

Type =**Sum(**
Click on cell B4
Type a colon :
Click on cell D4
Close the bracket by typing)
Press the **Enter** key

Editing cell contents

Cell D5 of 'ExcelExample1' currently contains the value 6,124. If you wish to change the value in that cell from 6,124 to 6,154 there are four options (you have already used the first method).

(a) Activate cell D5, type 6,154 and press **Enter**.

To undo this and try the next option press **Ctrl + Z**; this will always undo what you have just done (a very useful shortcut).

(b) **Double-click** in cell D5. The cell will keep its thick outline but you will now be able to see a vertical line flashing in the cell. You can move this line by using the direction arrow keys or the **Home** and the **End** keys. Move it to just after the 2, press the **backspace key** on the keyboard and then type 5. Then press **Enter**. (Alternatively, move the vertical line to just in front of the 2, press the **Delete** key on the keyboard, then type 5, followed by the **Enter** key).

When you have tried this press **Ctrl + Z** to undo it.

(c) **Click once** before the number 6,124 in the formula bar. Again, you will get the vertical line which can be moved back and forth to allow editing as in (b) above.

(d) Activate cell D4 and press **F2** at the top of your keyboard. The vertical line cursor will be flashing in cell D4 at the end of the figures entered there and this can be used to edit the cell contents, as above.

Deleting cell contents

There are a number of ways to delete the contents of a cell:

(a) Make the cell the active cell and press the **Delete** button. The contents of the cell will disappear.

(b) Go to the **Editing** section on the **Home** tab of the Ribbon. Click on the **Clear** button and various options appear. Click **Clear Contents**. You can also achieve this by **right-clicking** the cell and choosing **Clear contents**.

Any **cell formatting** (for example, cell colour or border) will not be removed when using either of these methods. To remove formatting click on the **Clear** button on the **Home** tab and select **Clear Formats**. If you want to remove both the formatting and the contents, click **Clear All**.

Ranges of cells

A range of cells can occupy a single column or row or can be a rectangle of cells. The extent of a range is defined by the rectangle's top-left cell reference and the bottom-right cell reference. If the range is within a single row or column, it is defined by the references of the start and end cells.

Defining a range is very useful as you can then manipulate many cells at once rather than having to go to each one individually.

The following shows that a rectangular range of cells has been selected from C4 to D6. The range consists of three rows and two columns.

	A	B	C	D	E	F
1	BUDGETED SALES FIGURES					
2		Jan	Feb	Mar	Total	
3		£'000	£'000	£'000	£'000	
4	North	2,431	3,001	2,189	7,621	
5	South	6,532	5,826	6,124	18,482	
6	West	895	432	596	1,923	
7	Total	9,858	9,259	8,909	28,026	
8						
9						

There are several ways of selecting ranges. Try the following:

(1) Click on cell C4, but hold the mouse button down. Drag the cursor down and to the right until the required range has been selected. Then release the mouse button. Now press the **Delete** key. All the cells in this range are cleared of their contents. Reverse this by **Ctrl+Z** and deselect the range by clicking on any single cell.

(2) Click on cell C4 (release the mouse button). Hold down the **Shift** key and press the **down** and **right-hand arrows** until the correct range is highlighted.

Deselect the range by clicking on any single cell.

(3) Click on cell C4 (release the mouse button). Hold down the **Shift** key and click on cell D6.

Deselect the range by clicking on any single cell.

(4) Say you wanted to select row 3, perhaps to change all the occurrences of £'000 to a bold font. Position your cursor over the figure 3 defining row 3 and click. All of row 3 is selected. Clicking on the **B** in the font group on the **Home** tab will make the entire row bold:

Whole spreadsheet selection

(5) Sometimes you may want to select every cell in the worksheet, perhaps to put everything into a different font:

Click on the triangle shape at the extreme top left of the cells (indicated above). Alternatively you can select the active cells using **Ctrl + A**.

There are a number of labour-saving shortcuts which allow you to quickly fill ranges of cells with headings (such as £'000, or month names) and with patterns of numbers. You can keep the 'ExcelExercise1' spreadsheet open throughout the following activities and simply open a new spreadsheet on which to experiment.

Illustration 2: Using the fill handle

(1) Create a new spreadsheet (**File tab>New.** Select **Blank workbook**.)

(2) Make cell B3 active and type Jan (or January) into it.

(3) Position the cursor at the bottom right of cell B3 (you will see a black **+** when you are at the right spot – this is often referred to as the **fill handle**).

(4) Hold down the mouse button and drag the cursor rightwards, until it is under row G. Release the mouse button.

The month names will automatically fill across.

(5) Using the same technique, fill B4 to G4 with £.

(6) Type 'Region' into cell 3A.

(7) Type the figure 1 into cell A5 and 2 into cell A6. Select the range A5–A6 and obtain the black cross at the bottom right of cell A6. Hold down the mouse key and drag the cursor down to row 10. Release the mouse button.

The figures 1–6 will automatically fill down column A.

Note. If 1 and 3 had been entered into A5 and C6, then 1, 3, 5, 7, 9, 11 would automatically appear. This does **not** work if just the figure 1 is entered into A5.

Percentages

Percentages can be calculated using a formula, or by using the percentage function. When using a formula always remember to multiply your answer by 100. For example, to calculate 40 out of 200 as a percentage value the formula would be = (40/200)*100

Alternatively, the percentage function can be used instead. Using the same figures as above simply enter =40/200 and this will show a decimal value.

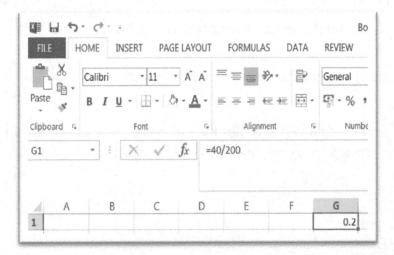

Then go to **Home**, **Number** and **Percentage**.

The decimal value will now be expressed as a percentage.

Copying and pasting formulas

You have already seen that formulas are extremely important in spreadsheet construction. In Excel it is very easy to define a formula once and then apply it to a wide range of cells. As it is applied to different cells the cell references in the formula are automatically updated. Say that, you wanted to multiply together each row of figures in columns A and B and to display the answer in the equivalent rows of column C.

Illustration 3: Copy and Paste

(1) Make C1 the active cell.

(2) Type **=**, then click on cell A1, then type ***** and click on cell B1.

(3) Press **Enter**.

The formula =A1*B1 should be shown in the formula bar, and the amount 232,800 should be shown in C1.

(4) Make C1 the active cell and obtain the black **+** by positioning the cursor at the bottom right of that cell.

(5) Hold down the mouse button and drag the cursor down to row 5.

(6) Release the mouse button.

Look at the formulas in column C. You will see that the cell references change as you move down the column, updating as you move from row to row.

	A	B	C	D
1	400	582	232800	
2	250	478	119500	
3	359	264	94776	
4	476	16	7616	
5	97	125	12125	

It is also possible to copy whole blocks of cells, with formulas being updated in a logical way.

(1) Make A1 the active cell and select the range A1:C5, for example, by dragging the cursor down and rightwards.

(2) Press **Ctrl+C** (the standard Windows Copy command) or click on the **Copy** symbol in the **Home** section of the ribbon.

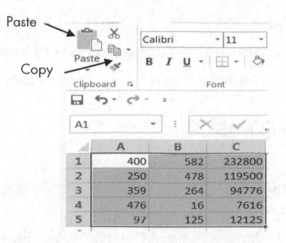

(3) Make E7 the active cell and press **Ctrl+V** or click on the **paste** button. E7 will become the top-right cell of the copied rectangle and will hold 400.

(4) Now, look at the formula shown in cell G7. It will show =E7*F7. So all cell references in the formulas have been updated relative to one another. This type of copying is called **relative copying**

(5) **Delete** the range E7:G7.

Sometimes you don't want to copy formulas and you only want to copy the displayed values. This can be done using **Paste special**.

Illustration 4: Paste special

Open the spreadsheet called 'Paste special example' from the files available for download at https://learningmedia.bpp.com/catalog?pagename=AAT_Spreadsheets.

You will see a simple inventory-type application listing quantities, prices and values. The values are obtained by formulas multiplying together prices and quantities. Say that you just want to copy the values of cells D3:D8, without the underlying formulas.

(1) Select the range D3:D8.

(2) Press **Ctrl+C** or the copy icon in the **Clipboard** part of **Home** on the Ribbon.

(3) **Right-click** on cell C12 to make it active, and choose **Paste Special** from the list.

(4) Check the **Values** radio button.

(5) Click **OK**.

The list of figures will be pasted, but if you look in the formula bar, you will see that they are just figures; there are no formulas there.

Note. If you change a quantity or price in the original table, the figures you have just pasted will not change; they have become pure numbers and do not link back to their source.

Cells can be linked between worksheets by copying and pasting links. This can be achieved by selecting, and copying the cell value that you wish to link, then go to **Home>Paste>Paste Link**.

Often you will need to insert or delete whole rows or columns in spreadsheets. This can easily be done and sometimes formulas are correctly updated – but they should always be checked. For this illustration we will go back to using the 'ExcelExample1' spreadsheet to insert and delete rows and columns.

Illustration 5: Using insert and delete

Close the spreadsheet you have recently been working on and go back to (using the tabs across the bottom of the screen) or reopen the spreadsheet 'ExcelExample1'.

Let us assume that we have a new region, East and that we want this to be in a row lying between North and South.

(1) Select row 5, by clicking on the 5, then click the right mouse button (right-click) and select **Insert**. You will see rows 5, 6 and 7 move down.

(2) Make B8 the active cell and you will see that the formula in the formula bar is =B4+B6+B7. If we were to put the figures for East into row 5 then those would not be correctly included in the total, though B5 has been updated to B6 etc.

(3) Reverse the last step (**Ctrl+Z**).

(4) Now, in cell B7 insert =SUM(B4:B6).

(5) Copy B7 across columns C7 to E7 (black cross and drag across).

(6) Check the formulas that are in cells C7 to E7 to ensure they have all been updated.

(7) Insert a whole row above row 5 (select row 5>right-click>**Insert**).

(8) Inspect the formulas in row 8, the new total row.

The formulas in the total row will now be showing =SUM(B4:B7), =SUM(C4:C7), etc. In this case the new row will be included in the total. Effectively, the range over which the totals are calculated has been 'stretched'. Depending how your copy of Excel is set up, you may notice little green triangles in row 8. If so, place your cursor on one and press the exclamation symbol. The triangles are warning that you have included empty cells in your total – not a problem here, but it might have been in some cases. Don't worry if the triangles aren't showing.

(9) Finally, delete row 5. Select the whole row by clicking on the 5, then right-click and choose **Delete** from the menu.

The cells below Row 5 will move up and the SUM formulas are again updated.

New columns can also be added. Say that we now wanted to include April in the results.

(1) Replace the current formula in E4 with =SUM(B4:D4).

(2) Copy the formula in E4 down through columns 5, 6 and 7. Check that the correct formulas are in cells E4–E7.

(3) Select column E, by clicking on the E, then click the right mouse button (right-click) and select **Insert**. You will see column E move to the right.

(4) Inspect the formulas now in Column F, the new total column.

You will see that the formula in F7 still says = SUM(B7:D7). It has **not been updated** for the extra column.

So, if an extra row or column is inserted in the middle of a range, the formula is updated because the new row or column probably (but not always) becomes part of the range that has to be added up.

However, if the extra row or column is added at the end of a range (or the start) the formula will not be updated to include that. That's reasonably logical as new items at the very start or end have a greater chance of being headings or something not part of the range to be included in a calculation.

Assessment focus point

Whenever columns or rows are added or deleted always check that formulas affected remain correct.

Changing column width and row height

You may occasionally find that a cell is not wide enough to display its contents. When this occurs, the cell displays a series of hashes ######. There are several ways to deal with this problem:

* Column widths can be adjusted by positioning the mouse pointer at the head of the column, directly over the little line dividing two columns. The mouse **pointer** will change to a **cross** with a double-headed arrow through it. Hold down the left mouse button and, by moving your mouse, stretch or shrink the column until it is the right width. Alternatively, you can double-click when the double-headed arrow appears and the column will automatically adjust to the optimum width.

* Highlight the columns you want to adjust and choose **Home>Cells>Format>Column Width** from the menu and set the width manually. Alternatively, you can right-click the highlighted column(s) and choose **Column Width** from the menu.

* Highlight the columns you want to adjust and choose **Home>Format>Autofit Column Width** from the menu and set the width to fit the contents.

Setting row heights works similarly.

Columns and rows can also be hidden from view by making the selection and going to **Home>Format>Hide & Unhide**.

Date and time stamps

Assessment focus point

Date and time stamps will not be an examined skill, however, we have left brief information here so you are aware how to use this in your working life.

You can insert the current date into a cell by **Ctrl+;** (semicolon)

You can insert the current time by **Ctrl+Shift +;**

You can insert date and time by first inserting the date, release **Ctrl**, press space, insert the time. The date can be formatted by going to **Home>Number>Date** and choosing the format required.

Naming cells and ranges

Illustration 6: Naming cells and ranges

(1) Open the worksheet called 'Name example'.

(2) Make cell B3 the active one and right-click on it.

(3) Select **Define name**.

(4) Accept the offered name, 'VAT' that Excel has picked up from the neighbouring cell.

(5) Highlight the range D4:D7, right-click **Define name** and accept the offered 'Net'.

(6) In E4 enter =Net*(1 + VAT).

(7) Copy E4 into E5:E7.

You will see the formula bar refers to names. This makes understanding a spreadsheet much easier.

A list of names can be seen using the **Formulas** section of the Ribbon and clicking on **Name Manager**

Merging cells

Instead of entering text or values (numbers) into one column you may wish to enter your data so that it is merged across a number of columns. To do this go to **Home>Alignment** and select:

A merged cell looks like this:

Merged cell

	A	B	C	D	E
1		Revenue			
2	Company	Jan	Feb	Mar	Apr
3	Annabel Limited	5000	5000	5000	5500
4	Beatrice & Co	12000	11500	13000	14000
5	Caroline Ltd	4000	3400	3500	4000
6	Delilah's Dressers	3000	4500	4000	4000

Keyboard shortcuts

Here are a few tips to quickly improve the **appearance** of your spreadsheets and speed up your work, using only the keyboard. These are all alternatives to clicking the relevant button in the **Home** section of the Ribbon.

To do any of the following to a cell or range of cells, first select the cell or cells and then:

(a)   Press **Ctrl + B** to make the cell contents **bold**.

(b)   Press **Ctrl + I** to make the cell contents *italic*.

(c)   Press **Ctrl + U** to underline the cell contents.

(d)   Press **Ctrl + C** to **copy** the contents of the cells.

(e)   Move the cursor and press **Ctrl + V** to **paste** the cell you just copied into the new active cell or cells.

(f)   'Toggle' between the two types of display by pressing **Ctrl +`** (the latter is the key above the **Tab** key). Press **Ctrl +`** again to go back to the previous display.

2 Spreadsheet construction

All spreadsheets need to be planned and then constructed carefully. More complex spreadsheet models should include some documentation that explains how the spreadsheet is set up and how to use it. When constructing a spreadsheet it is important to select valid, relevant and reliable data and this can come from a variety of sources.

There can be a feeling that, because the spreadsheet carries out calculations automatically, results will be reliable. However, there can easily be errors in formulas, errors of principle and errors in assumptions. All too often, spreadsheets offer a reliable and quick way to produce nonsense.

Furthermore, it is rare for only one person to have to use or adapt a spreadsheet and proper documentation is important if other people are to be able to make efficient use of it. To assist with spreadsheet construction, pre-designed templates can be used for purposes that may be common to multiple users. If a spreadsheet is of a specialist nature, or is being constructed for a one-off purpose, then the spreadsheet may be designed as bespoke or custom-made. Having the correct approach to spreadsheet construction can help ensure output meets user (or customer) requirements.

It is important to note that information has to be made available to users in a timely manner and communicated as appropriate. This is particularly important for financial information, where late delivery can result in penalties or other losses. This means that those who are responsible for spreadsheet construction need to observe any deadlines set, either by management or external agencies eg HM Revenue & Customs.

To help with communication and also branding, many organisations adopt a **house style** for their output. House style is a standardised set of rules of formatting to be used. Examples can include types of font, font size and text colour.

Assessment focus point

Look out for instructions on house style or formatting to be used on assessment tasks and always ensure that your formatting is consistent with the style requested.

The following should be kept in separate identifiable areas of the spreadsheet:

(1) An inputs and assumptions section, containing the variables (eg the amount of a loan and the interest rate, planned mark-ups, assumptions about growth rates).

(2) A calculations section, containing formulas.

(3) The results section, showing the outcome of the calculations.

Sometimes it is convenient to combine (2) and (3).

It is also important to:

(1) Document data sources. For example, where did the assumed growth rate come from? If you don't know that, how will you ever test the validity of that data and any results arising from it?

(2) Explain calculation methods. This is particularly important if calculations are complex or have to be done in a specified way.

(3) Explain the variables used in functions. Some functions require several input variables (arguments) and may not be familiar to other users.

(4) Set out the spreadsheet clearly, using underlinings, colour, bold text etc to assist users.

Illustration 7: Spreadsheet construction

Constructing a costing spreadsheet.

You want to set up a spreadsheet to record the time you and your colleagues spend on an assignment, and to cost it using your group's internal chargeout rates which are as follows:

Divisional chief accountant	£72.50
Assistant accountant	£38.00
Accounting technician (you)	£21.45
Secretary	£17.30

The spreadsheet needs to show the hours spent and costs per person, by week, for a three-week assignment. The time spent each week is shown below:

	Week 3	Week 2	Week 1
Divisional chief accountant	6 hrs 45 mins	4 hrs 30 mins	–
Assistant accountant	35 hrs	40 hrs	20 hrs
You	37 hrs 30 mins	40 hrs	32 hrs
Secretary	37 hrs 15 mins	32 hrs 15 mins	15 hrs

Setting up the assumptions area

As we will be referring to the chargeout rates for each week's costs, set these up in a separate area of the spreadsheet.

Headings and layout

Next we will enter the various **headings** required.

You want your spreadsheet to look like this:

	A	B	C	D	E	F	G
1	**Internal chargeout rates**						
2	Divisional chief accountant	£72.50					
3	Assistant accountant	£38.00					
4	Accounting technician	£21.45					
5	Secretary	£17.30					
6							
7	**Costs**	*Week 1*	*Week 2*	*Week 3*	*Total*		
8	Divisional chief accountant						
9	Assistant accountant						
10	Accounting technician						
11	Secretary						
12	**Total**						
13							
14	**Hours**	*Week 1*	*Week 2*	*Week 3*	*Total*		
15	Divisional chief accountant						
16	Assistant accountant						
17	Accounting technician						
18	Secretary						
19	**Total**						

Note the following points.

(a) Column A is wider to allow longer items of text to be entered. Depending on how your copy of Excel is set up, this might happen automatically or you may have to drag the line between the A and B columns to the right.

(b) We have used a **simple style for headings**. Headings tell users what data relates to and what the spreadsheet 'does'. We have made some words **bold**.

(c) **Numbers** should be **right-aligned** in cells. This usually happens automatically when you enter a number into a cell.

(d) We have left **spaces** in certain rows (after blocks of related items) to make the spreadsheet **easier to use and read**.

(e) Totals have been highlighted by a single line above and a double line below. This can be done by highlighting the relevant cells then going to the **Styles** group in the **Home** section of the Ribbon, clicking on the drop-down arrow and choosing the style you want, in this case '**Totals**'.

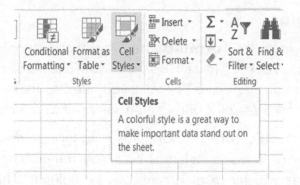

Alternatively, highlight the relevant cells, go to the **Font** area of the **Home** section and click on the drop-down arrow to access the list of **borders** available:

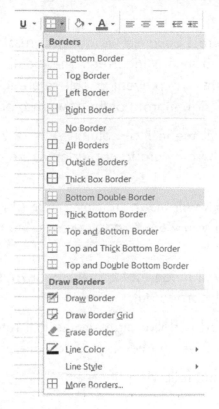

Entering data

Enter the time data in cells B15 to D18. Make sure you enter it correctly – the data is given to you in the order week 3 to week 1 but you would prefer it to be in the order week 1 to week 3. You will need to convert the time to decimal numbers.

	Hours	Week 1	Week 2	Week 3	Total
13					
14	Hours	Week 1	Week 2	Week 3	Total
15	Divisional chief accountant	0	4.5	6.75	
16	Assistant accountant	20	40	35	
17	Accounting technician	32	40	37.5	
18	Secretary	15	32.25	37.25	
19	Total				
20					
21					
22					
23					
24					

Inserting formulas

The next step is to enter the **formulas** required. For example, in cell B19 you want the total hours for Week 1. In cell B8 you want the total cost of time spent. You could enter this formula as =B15*B2, but you need to make sure that, as you copy the formula across for Weeks 2 and 3, you still refer to the chargeout rate in B2.

The quick way to insert a series of formulas is to type in the initial one and then to copy across a row or down a column. You may remember that cell references are cleverly updated as you move along the row or column. This was called **relative copying**. However, that will get us into trouble here. If cell B8 contains the formula =B15*B2 and that is copied one cell to the right, into column C, the formula will become =C15*C2.

The C15 reference is correct because we are progressing along the row, one month at a time, but the C2 reference is incorrect. The location of the chargeout rate does not move: it is **absolute**. To prevent a cell reference being updated during the copying process put a **$** sign in front of the row and/or column reference.

A reference like $A1 will mean that column A is always referred to as you copy across the spreadsheet. If you were to copy down, the references would be updated to A2, A3, A4, etc.

A reference such as A$1 will mean that row 1 is always referred to as you copy down the spreadsheet. If you were to copy across, the references would be updated to B1, C1, D1, etc.

A reference like $A$1 will mean that cell A1 is always referred to, no matter what copying of the formula is carried out.

The **function key F4** adds dollar signs to the cell reference, cycling through one, two or zero dollar signs. Press the **F4** key as you are entering the cell address.

You should end up with the following figures:

	B8			fx	=B15*$B$2		
	A	B	C	D	E	F	G
1	**Internal chargeout rates**						
2	Divisional chief accountant	£72.50					
3	Assistant accountant	£38.00					
4	Accounting technician	£21.45					
5	Secretary	£17.30					
6							
7	Costs	*Week 1*	*Week 2*	*Week 3*	Total		
8	Divisional chief accountant	0	326.25	489.375			
9	Assistant accountant	760	1,520	1,330			
10	Accounting technician	686.4	858	804.375			
11	Secretary	259.5	557.925	644.425			
12	Total						
13							
14	Hours	*Week 1*	*Week 2*	*Week 3*	Total		
15	Divisional chief accountant	0	4.5	6.75			
16	Assistant accountant	20	40	35			
17	Accounting technician	32	40	37.5			
18	Secretary	15	32.25	37.25			
19	Total						
20							
21							
22							
23							

Note that the formula in B8 refers to cell B15 (Week 1 hours) but to cell $B$2 – the absolute address of the chargeout rate.

The sales figure are untidy: some have comma separators between the thousands, some have one decimal place, some two. To tidy this up we will use the **Number** section of the Ribbon to format these numbers as **Currency**, and for the required **Decimal places** (two decimal places in this example). It is good practice to also format our results using **1000 separators**.

This drop-down provides more options, and is used in this example

(1) Select the range of cells B8:E12.

(2) Click in the small arrow just right of the word '**Number**' to open the **Format Cells** window.

(3) Select **Currency**, make sure the **Decimal places** reads 2 and that the £ symbol is showing.

You should see that all the figures in your spreadsheet are now in the same format.

(4) In cell E8, enter a formula to total the hours.

The spreadsheet should now be like this:

B8		fx	=B15*$B$2			
	A	B	C	D	E	F
1	**Internal chargeout rates**					
2	Divisional chief accountant	£72.50				
3	Assistant accountant	£38.00				
4	Accounting technician	£21.45				
5	Secretary	£17.30				
6						
7	**Costs**	*Week 1*	*Week 2*	*Week 3*	**Total**	
8	Divisional chief accountant	£0.00	£326.25	£489.38	£815.63	
9	Assistant accountant	£760.00	£1,520.00	£1,330.00	£3,610.00	
10	Accounting technician	£686.40	£858.00	£804.38	£2,348.78	
11	Secretary	£259.50	£557.93	£644.43	£1,461.85	
12	**Total**	**£1,705.90**	**£3,262.18**	**£3,268.18**	**£8,236.25**	
13						
14	**Hours**	*Week 1*	*Week 2*	*Week 3*	**Total**	
15	Divisional chief accountant	0	4.5	6.75	11.25	
16	Assistant accountant	20	40	35	95	
17	Accounting technician	32	40	37.5	109.5	
18	Secretary	15	32.25	37.25	84.5	
19	**Total**	**67**	**116.75**	**116.5**	**300.25**	
20						
21						
22						

And the formulas behind the cell contents should be:

6					
7	Costs	Week 1	Week 2	Week 3	Total
8	Divisional chief accountant	=B15*$B$2	=C15*$B$2	=D15*$B$2	=SUM(B8:D8)
9	Assistant accountant	=B16*$B$3	=C16*$B$3	=D16*$B$3	=SUM(B9:D9)
10	Accounting technician	=B17*$B$4	=C17*$B$4	=D17*$B$4	=SUM(B10:D10)
11	Secretary	=B18*$B$5	=C18*$B$5	=D18*$B$5	=SUM(B11:D11)
12	Total	=SUM(B8:B11)	=SUM(C8:C11)	=SUM(D8:D11)	=SUM(E8:E11)
13					
14	Hours	Week 1	Week 2	Week 3	Total
15	Divisional chief accountant	0	4.5	6.75	=SUM(B15:D15)
16	Assistant accountant	20	40	35	=SUM(B16:D16)
17	Accounting technician	32	40	37.5	=SUM(B17:D17)
18	Secretary	15	32.25	37.25	=SUM(B18:D18)
19	Total	=SUM(B15:B18)	=SUM(C15:C18)	=SUM(D15:D18)	=SUM(E15:E18)
20					
21					
22					

However, after designing the spreadsheet, you find out that the Divisional Chief Accountant has worked for 6 hours in week 4. He also wants you to add in to your calculations the costs of using two laptop computers, which were charged out at £100 per week each, for the first 3 weeks. You have also found out that the secretarial chargeout rate was increased by 10% in week 3. You now need to amend the spreadsheet to reflect these changes.

(1) Insert a column between columns D and E.

(2) Label E7 and E14 as Week 4.

(3) Enter the 6 hours in cell E15.

(4) Enter a formula in cell E8 to calculate the cost of these hours.

(5) Insert a row between rows 11 and 12.

(6) Enter Laptops in cells A6 and A12.

(7) In cell A22, enter Laptops and enter the number of laptops used each week.

(8) In cell B6 enter the cost of each laptop per week.

(9) Use a formula in cells B12 to D12 to calculate the cost of the laptops.

(10) Insert two rows between row 6 and 7.

(11) In cell B7, enter the percentage increase in the secretary's chargeout rate. Format this cell as percentage. Amend the formula in cell D13 accordingly.

(12) You may have noticed that the total cost and total hours total have not altered. This is because we have inserted rows and columns which were outside the range of the original formula used to calculate the totals. Amend your formulas accordingly.

Tidy the spreadsheet

The presentation is reasonable as we have taken care of it as we have developed the spreadsheet. This is good practice. You can now apply different formatting techniques – changing font colour or cell colour, for example. To change font colour, type (eg Arial) and size including **cell fill colour** or shading go to **Home>Font**. Save the spreadsheet as 'Costing Exercise-finished'.

The menu extract below indicates the **font type** is Calibri, and is in size 11. The **cell fill colour** icon is similar in appearance to a paint pot. The **font colour** can be changed by the drop down menu in the 'A' next to the cell fill colour icon.

Once you have tidied up your spreadsheet save the spreadsheet as 'Costing Exercise-finished'.

The spreadsheet should now look like this before updating cell F22 to include the Divisional chief accountant's week 4 hours:

| | F15 | ▾ | : | ✕ ✓ | fx | =SUM(F10:F14) | |

▲	A	B	C	D	E	F	G
1	**Internal chargeout rates**						
2	Divisional chief accountant	£72.50					
3	Assistant accountant	£38.00					
4	Accounting technician	£21.45					
5	Secretary	£17.30					
6	Laptop cost	£100.00					
7	Chargeout rate	10%					
8							
9	Costs	*Week 1*	*Week 2*	*Week 3*	*Week 4*	Total	
10	Divisional chief accountant	£0.00	£326.25	£489.38	£435.00	£1,250.63	
11	Assistant accountant	£760.00	£1,520.00	£1,330.00	£0.00	£3,610.00	
12	Accounting technician	£686.40	£858.00	£804.38	£0.00	£2,348.78	
13	Secretary	£259.50	£557.93	£708.87	£0.00	£1,526.29	
14	laptops	£200.00	£200.00	£200.00		£600.00	
15	Total	£1,705.90	£3,262.18	£3,332.62	£435.00	£9,335.69	
16							
17	Hours	*Week 1*	*Week 2*	*Week 3*	*Week 4*	Total	
18	Divisional chief accountant	0	4.5	6.75	6	17.25	
19	Assistant accountant	20	40	35		95	
20	Accounting technician	32	40	37.5		109.5	
21	Secretary	15	32.25	37.25		84.5	
22	Total	67	116.75	116.5	6	300.25	
23							
24	Laptops	2	2	2			
25							
26							
27							

And the formulas should look like this:

| | F15 | ▾ | : | ✕ ✓ | fx | =SUM(F10:F14) |

▲	A	B	C	D	E	F
1	**Internal chargeout rates**					
2	Divisional chief accountant	72.5				
3	Assistant accountant	38				
4	Accounting technician	21.45				
5	Secretary	17.3				
6	Laptop cost	100				
7	Chargeout rate	0.1				
8						
9	Costs	*Week 1*	*Week 2*	*Week 3*	*Week 4*	Total
10	Divisional chief accountant	=B18*$B$2	=C18*$B$2	=D18*$B$2	=E18*$B$2	=SUM(B10:E10)
11	Assistant accountant	=B19*$B$3	=C19*$B$3	=D19*$B$3	=E19*$B$2	=SUM(B11:E11)
12	Accounting technician	=B20*$B$4	=C20*$B$4	=D20*$B$4	=E20*$B$2	=SUM(B12:E12)
13	Secretary	=B21*$B$5	=C21*$B$5	=D21*($B$5+($B$5*$B$7))	=E21*($B$5+($B$5*$B$7))	=SUM(B13:E13)
14	laptops	=B24*$B$6	=C24*$B$6	=D24*$B$6		=SUM(B14:E14)
15	Total	=SUM(B10:B13)	=SUM(C10:C13)	=SUM(D10:D13)	=SUM(E10:E14)	=SUM(F10:F14)
16						
17	Hours	*Week 1*	*Week 2*	*Week 3*	*Week 4*	Total
18	Divisional chief accountant	0	4.5	6.75	6	=SUM(B18:E18)
19	Assistant accountant	20	40	35		=SUM(B19:D19)
20	Accounting technician	32	40	37.5		=SUM(B20:D20)
21	Secretary	15	32.25	37.25		=SUM(B21:D21)
22	Total	=SUM(B18:B21)	=SUM(C18:C21)	=SUM(D18:D21)	=SUM(E18:E21)	=SUM(B22:D22)
23						
24	Laptops	2	2	2		
25						
26						
27						

Illustration 8: Commission calculations

Commission calculations.

Four telesales staff each earn a basic salary of £14,000 pa. They also earn a commission of 2% of sales. The following spreadsheet has been created to process their commission and total earnings. **Give an appropriate formula for each of the following cells.**

(a) Cell D4
(b) Cell E6
(c) Cell D9
(d) Cell E9

	A	B	C	D	E
1	Sales team salaries and commissions - 200X				
2	Name	Sales	Salary	Commission	Total earnings
3		£	£	£	£
4	Northington	284,000	14,000	5,680	19,680
5	Souther	193,000	14,000	3,860	17,060
6	Weston	12,000	14,000	240	14,240
7	Easterman	152,000	14,000	3,040	17,040
8					
9	Total	641,000	56,000	12,820	68,820
10					
11					
12	Variables				
13	Basic Salary	14,000			
14	Commission rate	0.02			
15					

Solution

Possible formulas are:

(a) =B4*$B$14

(b) =C6+D6

(c) =SUM(D4:D7)

(d) There are a number of possibilities here, depending on whether you set the cell as the total of the earnings of each salesman (cells E4 to E7): =SUM(E4:E7) or as the total of the different elements of remuneration (cells C9 and D9): =SUM(C9:D9). Even better would be a formula that checked that both calculations gave the same answer. A suitable formula for this purpose would be:

=IF(SUM(E4:E7)=SUM(C9:D9),SUM(E4:E7),"ERROR")

We explain this formula after the next illustration, so don't worry about it at the moment!

Illustration 9: Actual sales and budgeted sales

Actual sales compared with budget sales.

A business often compares its results against budgets or targets. It is useful to express differences or **variations as a percentage of the original budget**: for example, sales may be 10% higher than predicted.

Continuing the telesales example, a spreadsheet could be set up as follows showing differences between actual sales and target sales, and expressing the difference as a percentage of target sales.

	A	B	C	D	E
1	Sales team comparison of actual against budget sales				
2	Name	Sales (Budget)	Sales (Actual)	Difference	% of budget
3		£	£	£	£
4	Northington	275,000	284,000	9,000	3.27
5	Souther	200,000	193,000	(7,000)	(3.50)
6	Weston	10,000	12,000	2,000	20.00
7	Easterman	153,000	152,000	(1,000)	(0.65)
8					
9	Total	638,000	641,000	3,000	0.47
10					

Give a suitable formula for each of the following cells.

(a) Cell D4
(b) Cell E6
(c) Cell E9

Try this for yourself, before looking at the solution.

Solution

(a) =C4 - B4

(b) =(D6/B6)*100

(c) =(D9/B9)*100. Note that in (c) you **cannot simply add up the individual percentage differences**, as the percentages are based on different quantities

3 Formulas with conditions ('IF' function)

Suppose the employing company in the above example awards a bonus to people who exceed their target by more than £1,000. The spreadsheet could work out who is entitled to the bonus.

To do this we would enter the appropriate formula in cells F4 to F7. For salesperson Easterman, we would enter the following in cell F7:

=IF(D4>1000,"BONUS"," ")

We will now explain this **IF** function.

IF statements follow the following structure (or 'syntax').

=IF(logical_test, value_if_true, value_if_false)

The **logical_test** is any value or expression that can be evaluated to Yes or No. For example, D4>1000 is a logical expression; if the value in cell D4 is over 1,000, the expression evaluates to Yes. Otherwise, the expression evaluates to No.

Value_if_true is the value that is returned if the answer to the **logical_test** is Yes. For example, if the answer to D4>1000 is Yes, and the value_if_true is the text string "BONUS", then the cell containing the IF function will display the text "BONUS".

Value_if_false is the value that is returned if the answer to the logical_test is No. For example, if the **value_if_false** is two sets of quote marks " " this means display a blank cell if the answer to the **logical_test** is No. So in our example, if D4 is not over 1,000, then the cell containing the IF function will display a blank cell.

Note the following symbols which can be used in formulas with conditions:

<	less than
<=	less than or equal to
=	equal to
>=	greater than or equal to
>	greater than
<>	not equal to

Care is required to ensure **brackets** and **commas** are entered in the right places. If, when you try out this kind of formula, you get an error message, it may well be a simple mistake, such as leaving a comma out.

Illustration 10: The IF function

Using the **IF** function.

A company offers a discount of 5% to customers who order more than £10,000 worth of goods. A spreadsheet showing what customers will pay may look like:

C8		fx	=IF(B8>$C$3,B8*$C$4,0)		
	A	B	C	D	E	F

	A	B	C	D
1	**Sales discount**			
2				
3	Discount hurdle		10,000	
4	Discount rate		5%	
5				
6	**Customer**	**Sales**	**Discount**	**Net price**
7		**£**	**£**	**£**
8	John	12,000	600	11,400
9	Margaret	9,000	0	9,000
10	William	8,000	0	8,000
11	Julie	20,000	1000	19,000
12				
13				
14				
15				

The formula in cell C8 is as shown: **=IF**(B8>$C$3, B8*$C$4, 0). This means, if the value in B8 is greater than £10,000 multiply it by the contents of C4, ie 5%, otherwise the discount will be zero. Cell D8 will calculate the amount net of discount, using the formula: =B8-C8. The same conditional formula with the cell references changed will be found in cells C9, C10 and C11.

Here is another illustration for you to try.

Illustration 11: The IF function

Open the spreadsheet called 'Exam Results' (one of the spreadsheets downloaded from https://learningmedia.bpp.com/catalog?pagename=AAT_Spreadsheets).

There are ten candidates listed, together with their marks.

The pass mark has been set at 50%.

See if you can complete column C rows 6 – 15 so that it shows PASS if the candidate scores 50 or above, and FAIL if the candidate scores less than 50.

Once it's set up and working correctly, change the pass mark in cell B3 to 60 and ensure that the PASS/FAIL indications reflect the change.

The formulas you need will be based on the one for cell C6.

C6			✗ ✓ fx	=IF(B6>=$B$3,"PASS","FAIL")		
▲	A	B	C	D	E	F
1	**Exam results**					
2						
3	Pass mark	50				
4						
5	**Candidate**	**Mark**	**Pass/fail**			
6	Alf	51	PASS			
7	Beth	56	PASS			
8	Charles	82	PASS			
9	David	42	FAIL			
10	Edwina	68	PASS			
11	Frances	36	FAIL			
12	Gary	75	PASS			
13	Hugh	53	PASS			
14	Iris	72	PASS			
15	John	34	FAIL			

Countif

The countif formula can be used to **count** how many cell values meet a specific criteria **IF** a condition is met.

Counta

The counta formula can be used to count the number of cells in a range that are not empty, and do not hold a value. Bear in mind that although a cell may appear blank technically it may not be empty as may contain a non-visible value.

The cells below in A1, A2 and A3 hold a non-visible value (apostrophes in this case)so there are three cells that are not empty.

The following **counta** formula will give the correct count of **3**.

	A
1	
2	
3	
4	=COUNTA(A1:A3)

Assessment focus point

In the assessment you may be asked to analyse and interpret data, including using forecasting tools. Make sure you understand how the different tools can be used and the most appropriate uses for them.

For example, our business in the above example may wish to know how many times sales have exceeded £10,000.

The answer here is twice, or **2** as both £12,000 and £14,000 are over £10,000. The following countif formula would calculate **2** as the result.

	A	B
1		**Sales £**
2	**Week 1**	8000
3	**Week 2**	12000
4	**Week 3**	9000
5	**Week 4**	14000
6		=COUNTIF(B2:B5,">10,000")

Compound (nested) IF functions

IF functions can also have multiple conditions within a formula meaning that two or more conditions need to be met for the calculation.

For example, a business may wish to give a 5% discount to customers who have made a sales order between £500 and £1,000. Here the **IF** function used would need to include two conditions for '>500' and '<1,000' and also be able to calculate the value of the 5% discount.

The following customers have made the following orders:

	A	B	C
1	**Customer**	**Order £**	**Discount £**
2	Cerise plc	450	
3	Green Ltd	800	
4	Plum Partners	1060	
5	Violet Ltd	900	

To calculate the discounts in column C the following **IF** formulas can be used:

	A	B	C
1	**Customer**	**Order £**	**Discount £**
2	Cerise plc	450	=IF((B2>500),(B2<1000))*B2*0.05
3	Green Ltd	800	=IF((B3>500),(B3<1000))*B3*0.05
4	Plum Partners	1060	=IF((B4>500),(B4<1000))*B4*0.05
5	Violet Ltd	900	=IF((B5>500),(B5<1000))*B5*0.05

To give the following results:

	A	B	C
1	**Customer**	**Order £**	**Discount £**
2	Cerise plc	450	0
3	Green Ltd	800	40
4	Plum Partners	1060	0
5	Violet Ltd	900	45

Note how two conditions have been included in one formula and these have to be met before the discount of 5% applies.

> **Assessment focus point**
>
> You may need to use a combination of different formulas to achieve an object set in the assessment, so be flexible and imaginative in how you can apply your spreadsheets skills. For example, in the above worksheet an **IF** Function can be used in column C to calculate discounts and also a **SUM** formula to total the order values in column B.

3.1 Conditional formatting

In addition to the condition determining whether PASS or FAIL appear, you can also conditionally format cell contents – for example, by altering the colour of a cell to highlight problems. This can be done by accessing the **Conditional Formatting** option in the **Styles** section of the **Home** tab of the Ribbon.

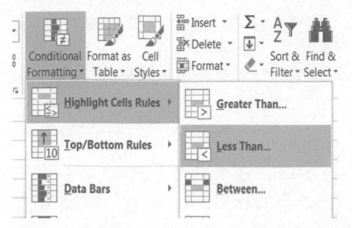

The marks which are less than the value in B3 have been highlighted by making the cell background red and the text white, as illustrated below:

	A	B	C
1	**Exam results**		
2			
3	Pass mark	50	
4			
5	**Candidate**	**Mark**	**Pass/fail**
6	Alf	51	PASS
7	Beth	56	PASS
8	Charles	82	PASS
9	David	42	FAIL
10	Edwina	68	PASS
11	Frances	36	FAIL
12	Gary	75	PASS
13	Hugh	53	PASS
14	Iris	72	PASS
15	John	34	FAIL

To produce the above result:

(1) Change the pass mark back to 50% if it is still at 60%.

(2) Highlight the numbers in column B.

(3) Click **Conditional formatting>Highlight cell rules>Less than**. You will see there are two white entry boxes.

(4) Click on cell B3. This will be entered automatically into the first box.

(5) Then click on the down arrow next to the second entry box. Click on **Custom format>Fill** and choose the red box. This changes the colour of the cell.

(6) Then click on **Font** and click the down arrow next to **Automatic**, under **Colour** and choose the white box.

(7) Click **OK**.

You can also use Conditional formatting to highlight the top three results, for example:

	A	B	C	D
1	**Exam results**			
2				
3	Pass mark	50		
4				
5	**Candidate**	**Mark**	**Pass/fail**	
6	Alf	51	PASS	
7	Beth	56	PASS	
8	Charles	82	PASS	
9	David	42	FAIL	
10	Edwina	68	PASS	
11	Frances	36	FAIL	
12	Gary	75	PASS	
13	Hugh	53	PASS	
14	Iris	72	PASS	
15	John	34	FAIL	
16				
17				
18				
19				
20				

To produce the above result:

(1) Highlight the numbers in column B.

(2) Click **Conditional formatting>Top/Bottom rules>Top 10 items**.

(3) In the first entry box, change the number from 10 to 3.

(4) In the second entry box, click on **Custom format>Fill** and choose the green box. This changes the colour of the cell.

(5) Then click on **Font** and click the down arrow next to **Automatic**, under **Colour** and choose the white box.

(6) Click **OK**.

3.2 Ranking data

Assessment focus point

Your skill requirement of ranking data is purely to have knowledge that it can be performed. You will not be asked to rank data in your live assessment.

The **RANK** function, one of Excel's statistical functions, ranks a number compared to other numbers in a list of data.

The syntax for the RANK function is:

= RANK (Number, Ref, Order)

Number – the cell reference of the number to be ranked.

Ref – the range of cells to use in ranking the Number.

Order – determines whether the Number is ranked in ascending or descending order. Use 0 for descending order and 1 for ascending order.

The names in the Exam Results spreadsheet are in alphabetical order. Say you want to keep them in that order but you want to see who came first, second, third etc. You can use RANK to give that information.

D6				fx	=RANK(B6,$B$6:$B$15,0)		
	A	B	C	D	E	F	G
1	Exam results						
2							
3	Pass mark	50					
4							
5	Candidate	Mark	Pass/fail	Rank			
6	Alf	51	PASS	7			
7	Beth	56	PASS	5			
8	Charles	82	PASS	1			
9	David	42	FAIL	8			
10	Edwina	68	PASS	4			
11	Frances	36	FAIL	9			
12	Gary	75	PASS	2			
13	Hugh	53	PASS	6			
14	Iris	72	PASS	3			
15	John	34	FAIL	10			
16							
17							

To produce the above result:

(1) Enter Rank in cell D5.

(2) In cell D6, type =RANK(B6,$B$6:$B$15,0). This means that B6 will be ranked within the range B6:B15 in descending order.

(3) Copy the formula to cells B7 to B15.

4 Charts and graphs

Charts and graphs are useful and powerful ways of communicating trends and relative sizes of numerical data in various outputs to meet equality of opportunity for users. Excel makes the production of charts relatively easy through the use of the chart wizard.

We will use the 'Sales discount' spreadsheet (one of the spreadsheets downloaded from https://learningmedia.bpp.com/catalog?pagename=AAT_Spreadsheets) to generate a number of different charts.

	A	B	C	D
1	**Sales discount**			
2				
3	Discount hurdle		10,000	
4	Discount rate		5%	
5				
6	**Customer**	**Sales**	**Discount**	**Net price**
7		£	£	£
8	John	12,000	600	11,400
9	Margaret	9,000	0	9,000
10	William	8,000	0	8,000
11	Julie	20,000	1000	19,000

First, we will generate a simple pie chart showing the total sales figure, before discounts.

Illustration 12: Pie charts

(1) Open the 'Sales discount' spreadsheet.

(2) Place your cursor on the word Customer, hold down the mouse button and drag the cursor downwards until you have selected the four names and four sales figures.

(3) Select the **Insert>Pie Chart icon** section from the Ribbon, then **3-D Pie**.

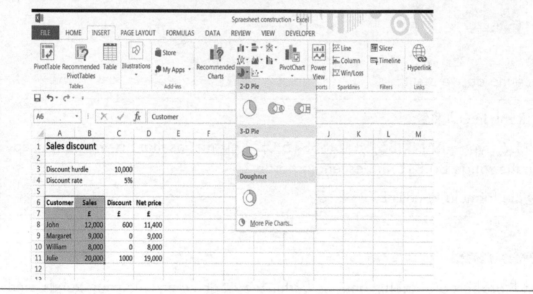

This will generate a pie chart that looks like this:

Sales £

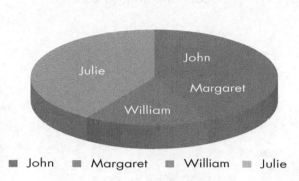

You will see that it already has a title, 'Sales £'. To make any changes to this, double-click the area where the title appears, then enter additional text or delete text you do not want. Below we have added 'for 20XX' and brackets around the pound sign.

Sales for 20XX (£)

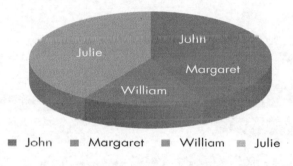

Changing the chart type

If you decide that a different chart may be more suitable for presenting your data you can easily change the chart type.

(1) Click on your chart. The **Chart Tools** options should become available at the top of the window.

(2) Click **Design>Change Chart Type**.

(3) From here, pick some charts from the following chart types to see what they produce: **3D, Bar, Column, Exploded, Line and Stacked.** For example the **stacked chart** will produce something like this:

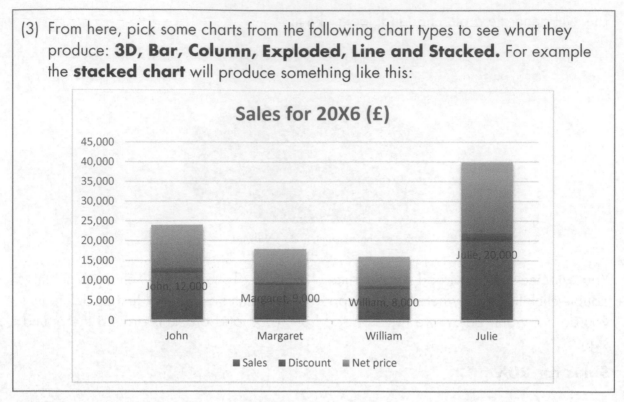

Bar charts

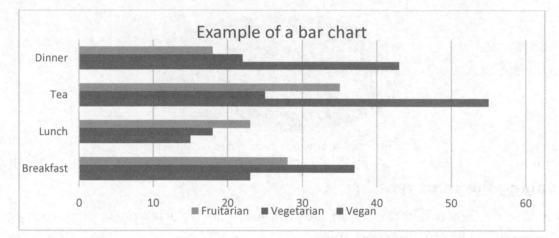

A pie chart is good for showing relative sizes of elements making up a total. However, sometimes you may want to be able to compare how two series of data are moving: sales and gross profit for example. In this case, bar charts (or line charts) are more suitable. Excel makes a distinction between bar charts that show vertical bars and those that show horizontal bars. **When the data is shown _vertically_ Excel refers to the chart as a _column_ chart, whereas if the data is shown _horizontally_ it is a _bar_ chart**.

Line chart

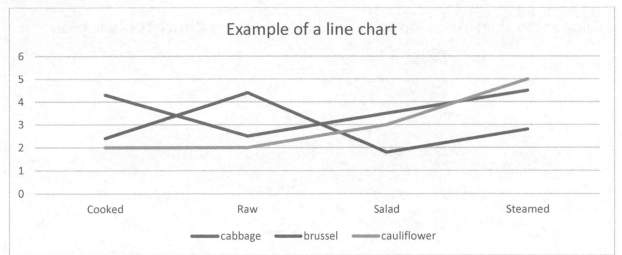

Example of a line chart

We are going to create a column chart showing the Sales and Net Price figure from the data on the 'Sales Discount' spreadsheet.

(1) Delete your chart by clicking on its outermost frame and pressing the **Delete** key.

(2) Place the cursor on the word Customer and drag the cursor down until all four names have been selected.

(3) Hold down the **Ctrl** key and select B6:B11. Still holding the **Ctrl** key down, select D6:D11.

(4) Release the mouse button and **Ctrl** key.

(5) On the Ribbon, choose **Insert>Column Chart icon>2D Column**.

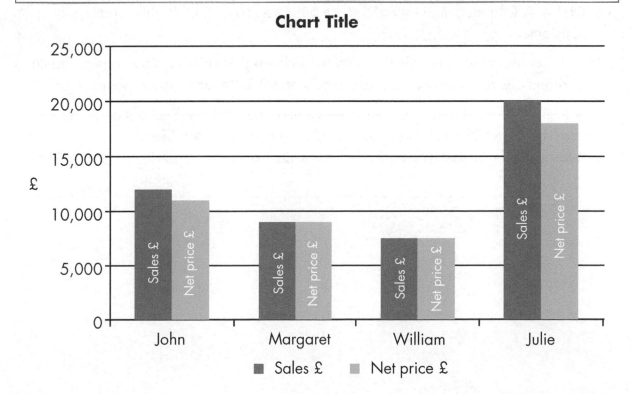

Chart Title

To change the chart title:

Click on the chart. At the top of the window you will see **Chart Tools** appear:

From the **Design** section, choose **Add Chart Element>Chart Title>Above Chart**. Type in 'Sales and Net Prices for 20XX (£)'.

To the bottom of the chart you will see a description for each column. This is called a Legend. You can move the legend by clicking on the Legend button.

You should also label the horizontal axis and the vertical axis.

(1) To label the horizontal axis, click **Design>Add Chart Element>Axis Titles>Primary Horizontal** (make sure you are clicked on the chart to see the **Chart Tools** tabs).

(2) The words 'Axis Title' appear at the bottom of the chart. Click on this, then press **Ctrl + A** to select all the words and type in your axis title, in this case 'Customer'.

(3) To label the other axis, this time choose **Primary Vertical**. You have a choice of directions for your text. Choose **Horizontal Title** and type a pound sign.

Note that if you are typing words for the vertical axis title the best option is usually **Horizontal Axis Title**. This can be completed through **Add Chart Elements>Axis Titles>More Axis Titles Options**. Try experimenting with that now.

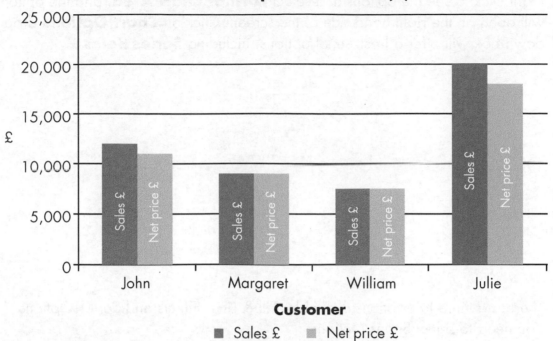

Sales and net prices in 20XX (£)

Exploded charts

These are useful when you want to highlight key areas of data within the chart itself

Using the spreadsheet 'Sales discount'

(1) Highlight the data to create a pie chart (cells A6:B11), click on **Insert>Charts** (you may have a **Recommended Charts** icon or a **pie chart icon**, either will work, you are aiming to create a pie chart initially)

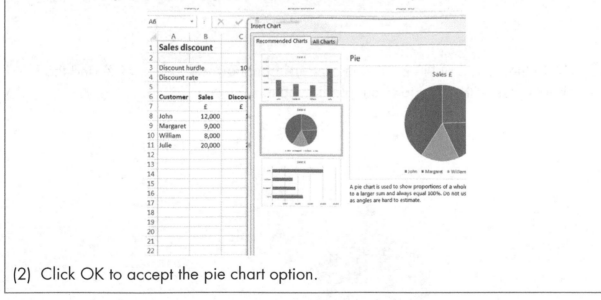

(2) Click OK to accept the pie chart option.

(3) Right click to see the options and select **Format Chart Area**, and the options will open on the right hand side of the screen. Click on **Chart Options** drop down box will offer a fresh set of options, including **Series Sales £.**

Format Data Seri... ▾ ×

SERIES OPTIONS ▾

◢ **SERIES OPTIONS**
Plot Series On
 ● Primary Axis
 ○ Secondary Axis
Angle of first slice

0°

Pie Explosion

0%

(4) There are three tab options available: Fill & Line, Effects and Series Options. You need to select Series Options:

Format Data Seri... ▾ ×

SERIES OPTIONS ▾

◢ **SERIES OPTIONS**
Plot Series On
 ● Primary Axis
 ○ Secondary Axis
Angle of first slice

0°

Pie Explosion

0%

(5) Go to the option of Pie Explosion, and using the arrows, select 10% and the chart's pies will all explode out of alignment:

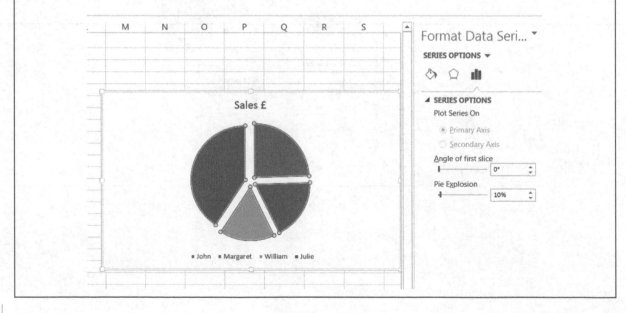

(6) If you want to select only one slice to explode, in order to highlight that particular piece of data, then you can simply click and slide the pie away from the others:

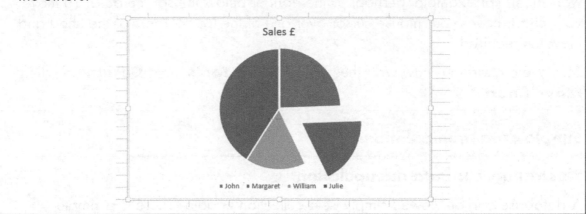

Formatting existing charts

Even after your chart is finished you can change it in a variety of ways.

(a) You can **resize it**, simply by selecting it and dragging out one of its corners.

(b) You can change the scale by dragging out the top, base or sides. To do so, hover your cursor over the four dots in the middle of the relevant top, base or side until your cursor turns into a **double-ended arrow**. Click and it will turn into a large cross, then drag with the mouse button still held down.

(c) You can change **each element** by **clicking** on it then selecting from the options available on the various **Chart tools** tabs.

(d) You can also select any item of text and alter the wording, size or font, or change the **colours** used, using the buttons on the **Font** section of the Home part of the ribbon. For example, practise increasing and decreasing the size of the font by clicking on the text you wish to change, then experimenting with the two different-sized capital A buttons:

(e) There is also a variety of colour schemes available from the Ribbon, under **Chart Tools>Design>Chart Styles**.

Assessment focus point

In the assessment you may need to move your chart to a specified location on the worksheet. For example, perhaps to the right or below the source data. To move your chart, hover your mouse cursor over one of the four corners of the chart and move as required.

To move a chart to a new worksheet select **Chart Tools**, then **Design** and then **Move Chart**.

Simple data manipulation

Illustration 13: Data manipulation

A database can be viewed simply as a collection of data. There is a simple database related to inventory, called 'Stockman Ltd' within the files downloaded from https://learningmedia.bpp.com/catalog?pagename=AAT_Spreadsheets. Open it now.

There are a number of features worth pointing out in this spreadsheet before we start data manipulation.

(1) Each row from 4–15 holds an inventory record.

(2) Column G makes use of the **IF** function to determine if the inventory needs to be reordered (when quantity < reorder level).

(3) In row 2, the spreadsheet uses automatic word wrap within some cells. This can improve presentation if there are long descriptions. To use word wrap, select the cells you want it to apply to, then click the **Wrap Text** icon in the **Alignment** section of the **Home** tab. The height of the cells needs to be increased to accommodate more than one line of text. To do this, select the whole row, then double-click on the line between the row numbers 2 and 3; or, instead, select **AutoFit Row Height** as shown below.

The data is currently arranged in part number order.

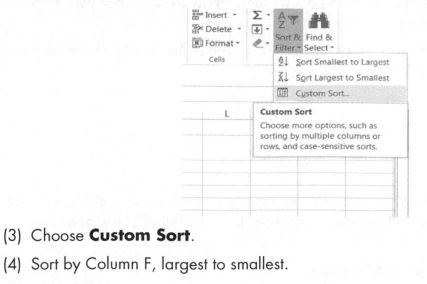

Wrap text in cell AutoFit Row Height

The horizontal rows are records: one record for each inventory type. The vertical columns are attributes (qualities) relating to each record.

Sorting the data

Let's say that we want to sort the data into descending value order.

(1) Select the data range A4:G15.

(2) At the right-hand side of the **Home** section of the Ribbon you will see the **Sort & Filter** drop-down menu.

(3) Choose **Custom Sort**.

(4) Sort by Column F, largest to smallest.

(5) Click **OK**.

You will see that the data has been sorted by value.

If you now **Sort by** Supplier (**Order A–Z**) you will have the data arranged by supplier and, within that, by value.

Sorting with multiple criteria

You may wish to sort your data using two more criteria (rather than by one column in the illustration above).

To sort data using multiple criteria within **Custom Sort** select **Add Level** to add additional sort criteria.

⁺A Z↓ Add Level	✕ <u>D</u>elete Level	☐ <u>C</u>opy Level	▲ ▼	<u>O</u>ptions...

> ### Assessment focus point
>
> You must be able to select the most appropriate chart or graph to summarise and present the information in the assessment. Remember to select tools such as labels, legends and the correct scale to answer the specific question. Being able to critically select and manipulate data is essential to success.

5 Printing

5.1 Printing spreadsheets

The print options for your spreadsheet may be accessed by selecting **File tab** and **Print**, or pressing **Ctrl + P**. Printing large spreadsheets without checking the print and layout settings will often result in printouts spread messily over several pages.

It is a good idea to preview your printout through **Print** to see what your printout will look like before printing.

A better option is to control what prints more precisely. This can be done from the **Page Layout** section of the Ribbon.

This allows you to, for example, print out selected areas only, include/exclude gridlines and the column and row headings, alter the orientation of the page and so on.

Scaling for printing or publication

The **Scale to Fit** section within **Page Layout** allows a worksheet to be scaled to a required size for printing or publication. Changing **Automatic** to **1 page** will mean all the data on that worksheet will be sized to one page.

Illustration 14: Page layout and printing

Open the spreadsheet we saw earlier called 'Costing Exercise – Finished'.

Assume that we only want to print out the cash flow without the table at the top showing the assumptions. We want to show the gridlines, but not the A, B, C... or 1, 2, 3... that head up columns and rows.

(1) Select the range A9:F24.

(2) Choose **Page Layout>Print Area>Set Print Area** from the Ribbon.

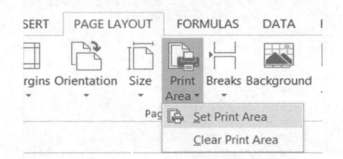

(3) Check the **Print Gridlines** box in **Page Layout>Sheet** options.

(4) Choose **File tab>Print**.

At this point you can check for obvious layout and formatting errors.

Spelling

Before you print, it is wise to check your work for spelling mistakes. To do this click the **Review** tab and select **Spelling**. If you have made any spelling errors Excel will offer alternative **Suggestions** which you can accept by clicking **Change** or ignore by clicking **Ignore** (**Once** or **All**).

If the word is, in fact, correct (for example, terminology that Excel does not recognise) you can add it to Excel's dictionary by clicking **Add to Dictionary**.

Preparing your spreadsheet for printing: Page set-up

The **Page Setup** area of the **Page Layout** tab on the Ribbon also allows you to specify certain other details that affect how your spreadsheet looks when it prints out.

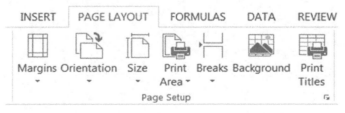

From here you can set the size of the **Margins** (the white spaces that print around the spreadsheet) and choose whether to print the spreadsheet in landscape **Orientation** (ie wider than tall) rather than the default portrait **Orientation** (taller than wide).

If you want to make sure that your spreadsheet will print onto one page, you can choose to **Fit to** 1 page wide by 1 page tall. This can be done by accessing the **Page Setup** options, by clicking on the little arrow in the bottom-right corner of the section on the ribbon.

Print settings can also be accessed through the **File tab**.

Imagine you are printing out a spreadsheet that will cover several pages. It is important that certain information is present on each page. For example:

- The spreadsheet title
- The page number and total pages
- The author
- The row and column headings

This can be done by accessing the **Page Setup** options, in the way outlined above, or by clicking on the **Print Titles** icon.

Headers appear at the top of each page. For example, a custom header could be:

Author   Budget for 2013   Date printed

Footers appear at the bottom of each page, for example:

Page   File name

The **Sheet** tab allows you to specify the rows and columns to be repeated on each page. For example, you might want to repeat the months across the top of each page and the type of income down the left of each page.

We have provided a demonstration spreadsheet in the downloaded files, 'Print practice'. Open it and try the following:

Insert a **Header**: Author name, Title (Budget 2013) Date printed

Insert a **Footer**: Page number, File name

Click **Page setup** (or **Print Titles**)>**Header/Footer**> **Custom Header** and **Custom Footer**.

Ensure that the headings in column A are repeated on the second page.

Use this spreadsheet to insert page breaks (**Breaks**) and other remaining options in the **Page Setup** area to:

- Insert the current filename in the bottom centre of the page
- Ensure page numbers are inserted top right of the page
- Insert a date and time in the top left of the page

Assessment focus point

Always look out for instructions on the assessment for entering headers and footers and always enter them using the appropriate information and the correct location on the page. Remember your audience in the preparation of any report, so consider using summary sheets, hiding unnecessary rows/columns and adding labels to ensure clarity. You will not be asked to insert page breaks or page numbers, but these are included to enhance your business knowledge of Excel.

Printing formulas

Occasionally, perhaps for documentation or checking, you might want the spreadsheet formulas to be printed out instead of the calculated results of the formula. To do this:

(1) Display the formulas on the screen by pressing **Ctrl +`** (or **Formulas** in the ribbon and **Show formulas**)

(2) Set the area you want to be printed: **Page Layout>Print Area>Set Area**

(3) Check what the printout will look like: **File tab>Print**.

(4) Adjust as necessary and print out when happy with the display

Printing charts

Charts can be printed either with or without the data on the worksheet.

To print only the chart, simply click on it and then press **Ctrl + P**. As always it is wise to preview through the **File tab** first.

If you also want to print the worksheet data, click away from the chart into any cell. Preview to make sure that the chart is the right size and is in the right position. Then press **Ctrl + P**.

Annotating output

You may wish to add information to your spreadsheets by using **comment boxes** annotate worksheets. Comment boxes can be added through **Review>New Comment.** Comment boxes can also be hidden through the **Review** tab if you prefer your annotations to be out of sight.

Charts and graphs can be annotated by using **Text Boxes**. To use this technique select **Insert>Text>Text Box**. You can then drag your text box to any location on your chart or graph.

Chapter summary

- A **spreadsheet** is basically an electronic piece of paper divided into **rows** and **columns**. The intersection of a row and a column is known as a **cell**.

- Essential basic **skills** include how to **move around** within a spreadsheet, how to **enter** and **edit** data, how to **fill** cells, how to **insert** and **delete** columns and rows and how to improve the basic **layout** and **appearance** of a spreadsheet.

- **Relative** cell references (eg B3) change when you copy formulas to other locations or move data from one place to another. **Absolute** cell references (eg $B$3) stay the same.

- A wide range of **formulas** and functions are available within Excel. We looked at the use of conditional formulas that use an **IF** statement.

- A spreadsheet should be given a **title** which clearly defines its purpose. The contents of rows and columns should also be clearly **labelled**. **Formatting** should be used to make the data in the spreadsheet easy to read and interpret.

- **Numbers** can be **formatted** in several ways, for instance with commas, as percentages, as currency or with a certain number of decimal places.

- Excel includes the facility to produce a range of charts and graphs. The **Chart Wizard** provides a tool to simplify the process of chart construction.

- Spreadsheets can be **printed** and the **Print Preview** function can be used to see what a printout will look like before actually printing.

- Spreadsheets can be used in a variety of accounting contexts. You should practise using spreadsheets; **hands-on experience** is the key to spreadsheet proficiency.

- **Absolute (reference):** A cell reference that does not change and is particularly useful when copying a formula across data

- **Bar chart:** A chart where data is grouped into 'bars', customarily used to show relative size between groups

- **Conditional formatting:** Allows users to format cells depending on specified conditions

- **Copying and pasting formulas:** A technique using an existing formula to quickly apply to different cell references within a spreadsheet

- **Fill handle:** A black cursor sign **+** that indicates it is possible to drag the cursor to infill cells

- **Formulas:** Used in calculating a range of requested values

- **IF function:** A logical function that calculates a value or outcome depending on specified conditions

- **House style:** A standardised style of formatting adopted by organisations

- **Orientation:** Describes the style of presentation or printing set-up chosen, ie landscape or portrait

- **Page layout:** Allows users to print specific areas of a worksheet

- **Paste special:** Used when copying values instead of formulas

- **Pie chart:** A circular chart displaying segments of data

- **Print preview:** Allows users to see what the printout will look like before printing

- **Ranking data:** A statistical function that ranks or classifies the size of a number compared to other numbers in the same list

- **Relative copying:** A cell reference that does change when copying a formula across data

- **Summary sheet:** A worksheet that links to other data or worksheets

- **Workbook:** A spreadsheet that consists of one or more worksheets

- **Worksheet:** Individual spreadsheet pages contained in a workbook

Test your learning

1 **List three types of cell contents.**

2 **What do the F5 and F2 keys do in Excel?**

3 **What technique can you use to insert a logical series of data such as 1, 2 .... 10, or Jan, Feb, March, etc?**

4 **How do you display formulas instead of the results of formulas in a spreadsheet?**

5 **List five possible changes that may improve the appearance of a spreadsheet.**

6 **What is the syntax (pattern) of an IF function in Excel?**

7 The following spreadsheet shows sales of two products, the Ego and the Id, for the period July to September.

	A	B	C	D	E
1	Sigmund Ltd				
2	Sales analysis - quarter 3, 2010				
3		July	August	September	Total
4	Ego	3,000	4,000	2,000	9,000
5	Id	2,000	1,500	4,000	7,500
6	Total	5,000	5,500	6,000	16,500

Devise a suitable formula for each of the following cells.

(a) Cell B6

(b) Cell E5

(c) Cell E6

8 The following spreadsheet shows sales, exclusive of VAT, the VAT amounts and the VAT inclusive amounts. The old VAT rate of 17.5% has been used and needs to be updated to the new 20% rate. It is important that this can easily be changed without needing to change any of the formulas in the spreadsheet.

	A	B	C	D
1	Taxable Supplies Ltd	Vat rate		0.175
2				
3		January	February	March
4	Product A	5,000	4,000	3,000
5	Product B	2,000	1,500	4,000
6	Product C	7,000	5,700	4,000
7	Product D	2,000	3,000	1,000
8	Product E	1,000	2,400	6,000
9	Total net	17,000	16,600	18,000
10	VAT	2,975	2,905	3,150
11	Total gross	19,975	19,505	21,150

Suggest suitable formulas for cells:

(a) B9

(b) C10

(c) D11

More advanced spreadsheet techniques (Excel 2013)

Learning outcomes

1.2	**Securely store and retrieve relevant information**
	Students need to be able to:
	• Securely store, backup, archive and retrieve data in line with local policies
	• Rename files in line with local conventions
2.2	**Accurately enter data**
	Students need to know:
	• Why their own data input needs to be accurate
	• Why they may need to select relevant data from different sources and where to paste that data in their spreadsheet
	Students need to be able to:
	• Manually enter data accurately
	• Link data from different sources and across different worksheets
	• Remove duplications in data
	• Import data
3.1	**Select and use a range of appropriate formulas and functions to perform calculations**
	Students need to be able to:
	• Plan, select and use a range of formulas to manipulate and analyse the data
	• Plan, select and use appropriate mathematical and logical functions and statistical techniques

3.2	**Select and use relevant tools to analyse and interpret data**
	Students need to be able to:
	• Assess and select the correct analysis tool for a given task • Analyse data using multiple sorting criteria • Analyse data using multiple filtering criteria • Use Conditional Formatting to enhance decisions • Analyse data using pivot tables and charts • Remove duplicates • Use lookup tables • Select and use appropriate forecasting tools • Summarise data using sub totals
3.4	**Edit and update data**
	Students need to be able to:
	• Change existing data • Include relevant new data in a spreadsheet • Identify and remove any further duplicates • Update relevant new data in a chart
4.1	**Use appropriate tools to identify and resolve errors**
	Students need to be able to:
	• Use formula auditing tools • Select and use error checking tools • Show the formulas within a spreadsheet
4.2	**Assess that new data has been accurately added**
	Students need to be able to:
	• Consider if any new data added to the spreadsheet is included in the analysis • Check new data is fully included in an existing chart
4.3	**Protect integrity of data**
	Students need to know:
	• Why protection of the integrity of their data is important • Why they may need to use and share spreadsheet passwords • With whom they can share spreadsheet passwords
	Students need to be able to:
	• Use data validation to restrict editing • Protect cells and worksheets • Use passwords • Keep data secure from unauthorised use

Assessment context

The advanced techniques covered in this chapter are not covered elsewhere on any other units and you may find some of these techniques completely new to you.

Qualification context

This chapter goes into some detail on the use of passwords to protect access to work and may recall from earlier studies the importance of data protection to maintain confidentiality of sensitive information.

Business context

The more advanced spreadsheet techniques can help management make better business decisions by drilling down through data and applying the various data analysis functions available on spreadsheet software.

Chapter overview

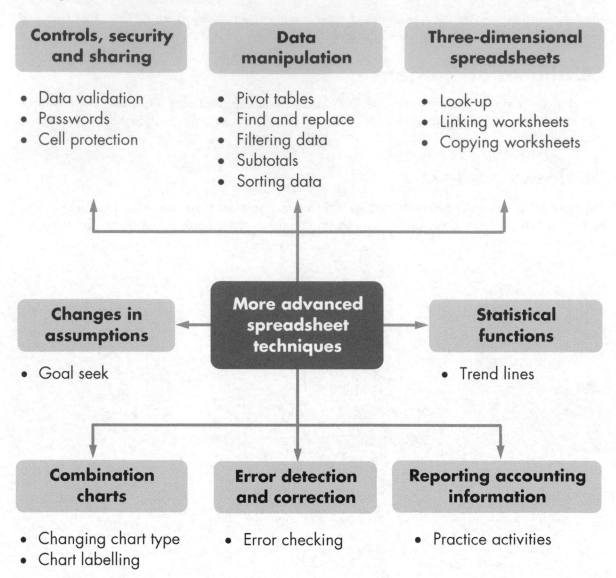

Controls, security and sharing

- Data validation
- Passwords
- Cell protection

Data manipulation

- Pivot tables
- Find and replace
- Filtering data
- Subtotals
- Sorting data

Three-dimensional spreadsheets

- Look-up
- Linking worksheets
- Copying worksheets

More advanced spreadsheet techniques

Changes in assumptions

- Goal seek

Statistical functions

- Trend lines

Combination charts

- Changing chart type
- Chart labelling

Error detection and correction

- Error checking

Reporting accounting information

- Practice activities

Introduction

In this chapter, we build upon the knowledge and skills covered in the preceding introductory chapter and look at advanced spreadsheet techniques, enabling users to manipulate data even further to assist in decision making and reporting.

1 Controls, security and sharing

1.1 Backups, passwords and cell protection

There are facilities available in spreadsheet packages which can be used as controls – to prevent unauthorised or accidental amendment or deletion of all or part of a spreadsheet. There are also facilities available for hiding data, and for preventing (or alerting users about) incorrect data.

Saving files and backing up

(a) **Save.** When working on a spreadsheet, save your file regularly, as often as every ten minutes, using **File tab>Save** or pressing **Ctrl + S**. This will prevent too much work being lost in the event of a system crash.

Save files in the appropriate **folder**, this may be on your hard drive (computer), or on the local network or, increasingly, files can be saved remotely. Businesses are increasingly using 'cloud' (or internet) based storage, such as Amazon, OneDrive (Microsoft), Google, Dropbox etc.

If a new location needs to be added to the storage on the computer, it is possible to click on Add a place (to add a new location) so that they are easy to locate. If you need to save the file to a new folder, select the required location and use the **New folder** option.

Give the folder a suitable name (for example, the name of the client you are working on or following your employer's standard naming practice or other local conventions).

Even the cloud based storage options allow links to be set up using the Explorer tool. Here is an example using Dropbox.

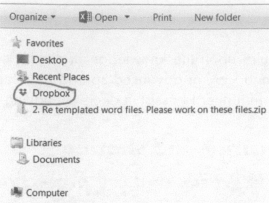

(b) **Save as**. A simple **save** overwrites the existing file. If you use **Save as** then you can give the file a different name, preserving previous versions. For example, **Save as** 'Budget Edition 1', 'Budget Edition 2', 'Budget Edition 3'. This is much safer than simply relying on the most recent version – which might be beyond fixing! When saving files it is also possible to save work in other file formats other than spreadsheets. These can include comma-separated values (CSV) and portable document format, more commonly known as pdf.

CSV files are plain text files, but which have markers (commas) which separate (delimit) the fields of data. This can aid conversion to spreadsheets or other applications. They are used when information needs to be exchanged between difference applications. Complex data can be downloaded into the CSV, then opened in a new application.

PDF files are particularly useful when you want the 'look' of a file to be exact. It takes an electronic image of the file, allowing navigation and printing of the file, without the user necessarily having to have the same original software. For example, you may convert an Excel spreadsheet to pdf, allowing the recipient to view the data (even if they do not have Microsoft Excel on their computer).

Assessment focus point

In the assessment it is likely you will need to download a data file, and then **rename** this file as requested in the assessment instructions. Always follow file renaming instructions accurately, and carefully!

(c) **Backups.** Because data and the computers or storage devices on which it is stored can easily be lost or destroyed, it is vital to take regular copies or backups. If the data is lost, the backup copy can be used to **restore** the data up to the time the backup was taken. Spreadsheet files should be included in standard backup procedures, for example the daily backup routine.

The backups could be held on a separate external hard drive, or perhaps a USB memory stick; they should be stored away from the original data, in case there is a fire or other disaster at the organisation's premises. Alternatively, the backups can be saved to a network location. Some backups are now stored on the internet ('the cloud').

(d) **AutoRecover.** Excel has a built-in feature that saves copies of all open Excel files at a fixed time interval. The files can be restored if Excel closes unexpectedly, such as during a power failure.

Turn on the **AutoRecover** feature by clicking **File tab>Excel Options>Save**.

The default time between saves is every 10 minutes. To change this, click the **Save AutoRecover info every** checkbox and enter any number of minutes between 1 and 120.

In the **AutoRecover file location** box, you can type the path and the folder name of the location in which you want to keep the AutoRecover files.

Protection

(a) **Cell protection/cell locking.** This prevents the user from inadvertently changing cells that should not be changed. There are two ways of specifying which cells should be protected.

(i) All cells are locked, except those specifically unlocked.

This method is useful when you want most cells to be locked. When protection is implemented, all cells are locked unless they have previously been excluded from the protection process. You will also see here a similar mechanism for hiding data. In this way specified **ranges** of cells can be locked and unlocked.

Illustration 1: Protecting worksheets

(1) Open the spreadsheet 'Costing Exercise–Finished'.

(2) Highlight the range B2:B5. This contains some of the assumptions on which the cash flow forecast is based and this is the only range of cells that we want to be unlocked and available for alteration.

(3) In the **Home** section of the Ribbon, click on the small arrow beside **Fonts** and then choose **Protection**.

(4) Untick the **Locked** and **Hidden** boxes.

(5) Click on **OK**.

(6) Now go to the **Review** group on the Ribbon.

(7) Click on **Protect Sheet**.

(8) Don't enter a password when prompted, simply click **OK**.

Now investigate what you can change on the spreadsheet. You should find that only cells B2:B5 can be changed. If you try to change anything else, a message comes up telling you that the cell is protected.

Click on **Unprotect Sheet** to make every cell accessible to change again.

(ii)   Most are unlocked, except those specified as being locked.

This method is useful if only a few cells have to be locked.

Illustration 1 (continuation): Protecting worksheets

(1) Open the spreadsheet 'Sales discount'.

(2) Assume that we want to lock only the 10,000 in cell C3 and the 5% figure in cell C4.

(3) Select the whole spreadsheet and, as we did above, click on the small arrow beside **Fonts**. Then choose **Protection** and untick the **Locked** and **Hidden** boxes. The cells can still be changed if you do not do this step.

(4) Select the range of cells C3:C4.

(5) In the **Home** section of the Ribbon go to the **Cells** group and click on **Format**.

(6) Click on **Lock Cell**.

(7) Click on **Protect Sheet** from the same **Format** menu. The cells remain editable if you do not do this step.

You are offered the chance to enter a password.

Now you will be prevented from changing just those two cells.

(8) **Hiding and showing formulas** – the same process can be used to hide or show formulas on a worksheet by selecting **Hidden** within **Protection** to hide formulas, and deselect **Hidden** to allow formulas to be seen by users.

(b)   **Passwords.** There are two levels of password.

(i)   All access to the spreadsheet can be protected and the spreadsheet encrypted. This can be done by:

(1) **File button>Info>Protect Workbook>Encrypt with Password**.

(2) You are then asked to enter, and verify, a password. Heed the warning: if you forget the password, there's no likelihood of recovery of the spreadsheet.

(3) To remove the password protection use:

File button>Info>Protect Workbook>Encrypt with Password

(4) Then delete the asterisks in the password box and click OK.

(ii) The spreadsheet can be password-protected from amendment, but can be seen without a password. This can be done as follows:

(1) **File tab>Info>Protect Workbook>Protect Current Sheet**

(2) Select the level of access allowed to users.

(3) In the **Password to modify** box type a password, then retype it to confirm and click **OK**.

(4) Click **Save**.

Now, if you close the file and re-open it, you will be asked for a password to get full access; without the password you can open it in read-only mode, so that it can be seen but not changed.

To keep the integrity of a password system, passwords should be kept private and not shared with others. There may sometimes be a need for passwords to be shared between two or more persons. This may be due to a wider access of information that is not of a sensitive nature. If this is the case then organisational policies will need to be adhered to so that access is restricted to those with proper authorisation. An additional level of security may require more frequent changes of passwords when there are multiple users of one password.

1.2 Data validation

Sometimes only a specific type or range of data is valid for a certain cell or cells. For example, if inputting hours worked in a week from a time sheet, it could be known that no one should have worked more than 60 hours. It is possible to test data as it is input and to either prevent input completely, or simply warn that the input value looks odd. This is known as 'data validation' or 'data restriction'. Errors or warnings can also be shown by circling invalid data in red.

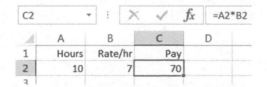

In this simple spreadsheet, C2 holds the only formula; A2 and B2 are cells into which data will be entered, but we want the data to conform to certain rules:

Hours <= 60. If greater than 60, a warning is to be issued.

Rate/hr >=8 and <=20. Data outside that range should be rejected.

Illustration 2: Data validation

(1) Set up a new spreadsheet with the above data and make A2 the active cell. Go to **Data>Data Validation** (in **Data Tools** section).

(2) Under the **Data Validation Settings** tab, **Allow Decimal**, select **less than or equal to** from the drop-down list and enter 60 as the **Maximum**.

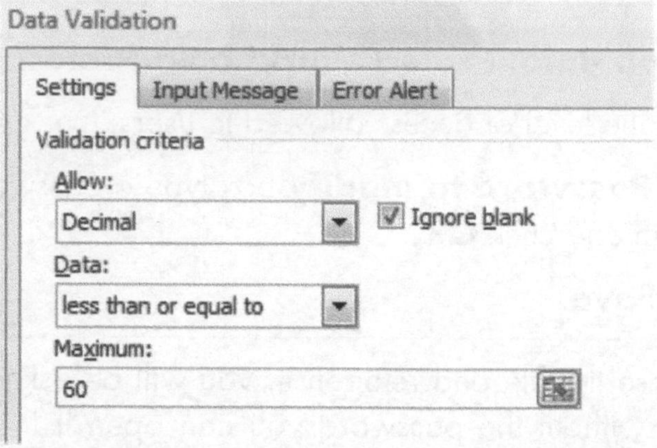

(3) Under the **Input Message** tab enter 'Warning' as the title and 'Hours expected to be less than 60' as the input message.

(4) Under the **Error Alert** tab change the **Style** to Warning, enter 'Attention' as the title and 'Check hours: look too large' as the **Error message**.

(5) Click **OK**.

(6) Now try to enter 70 into A2. You will first see an information message explaining what data is expected, then a warning message and the option to continue.

(7) Now try to set up cell B2 with appropriate messages and to prevent any value outside the range 8–20 from being entered at all.

Assessment focus point

In addition to Error Alerts and Error messages the data validation function can also be used to apply circles to highlight invalid data. To apply circles to your data follow the same routine as above and then select **Circle Invalid Data** from the data validation drop down menu. You need to be aware that these circles can be applied, however, you won't be asked to apply them.

2 Data manipulation

Data manipulation refers to a number of techniques available in Excel for summarising, analysing and presenting data.

Sorting the data

Data can be sorted into ascending or descending numeric order, or alphabetically A-Z or Z-A, from the **Sort & Filter** drop-down menu. A feature here is **Custom Sort** and this allows sorting to be completed on a specified column.

When numeric data has been sorted into groups Excel can calculate a **Subtotal** of each group by selecting **Data>Subtotal**.

Illustration 3: Subtotals

(1) Open a new spreadsheet and enter the following information:

	A	B	C
1	Area	Sales	
2	A	30	
3	A	20	
4	B	90	
5	B	10	
6			

(2) Select cell references A1 to B5.

(3) Select **Data>Subtotals**.

(4) You should see:

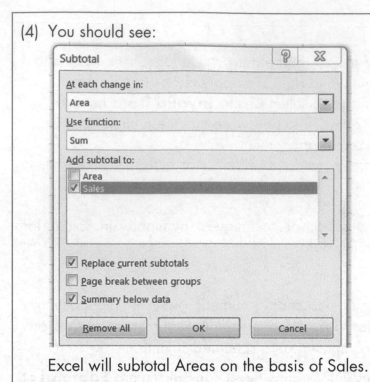

Excel will subtotal Areas on the basis of Sales.

(5) Click **OK**.

(6) You should see:

	A	B	C
1	Area	Sales	
2	A	30	
3	A	20	
4	**A Total**	50	
5	B	90	
6	B	10	
7	**B Total**	100	
8	**Grand Total**	150	
9			

Areas A and B have been subtotalled 50 and 100 respectively with an overall Grand Total of 150.

Subtotal formulas

Subtotals can also be calculated using formulas. Popular subtotal formulas include; average, maximum, minimum and a sum of values from a range of data.

Different calculations use an **'operation code'**. An operation code is a specific number inserted within a formula to request Excel to perform a particular operation, for example the number '1' denotes an average calculation. Other operation codes that can be used in a **subtotal** formula include:

Operation	Operation code
1	AVERAGE
4	MAXIMUM
5	MINIMUM
9	SUM

For example, a business has made the following weekly sales units:

	A	B
1		**Sales units**
2	Monday	240
3	Tuesday	300
4	Wednesday	320
5	Thursday	280
6	Friday	300
7	Saturday	440
8	Sunday	360
9		
10	**Average**	
11	**Maximum**	
12	**Minimum**	
13	**Sum**	

The business wishes to calculate the average, maximum, minimum and sum of the range of data using subtotals the following operational codes and formulas can be used:

	A	B
1		**Sales units**
2	Monday	240
3	Tuesday	300
4	Wednesday	320
5	Thursday	280
6	Friday	300
7	Saturday	440
8	Sunday	360
9		
10	**Average**	=SUBTOTAL(1,B2:B8)
11	**Maximum**	=SUBTOTAL(4,B2:B8)
12	**Minimum**	=SUBTOTAL(5,B2:B8)
13	**Sum**	=SUBTOTAL(9,B2:B8)

The calculated values are:

	A	B
1		**Sales units**
2	Monday	240
3	Tuesday	300
4	Wednesday	320
5	Thursday	280
6	Friday	300
7	Saturday	440
8	Sunday	360
9		
10	**Average**	320
11	**Maximum**	440
12	**Minimum**	240
13	**Sum**	2240

Filtering the data

Filtering data allows you to select and display just some of it in the table. This is useful if the table consists of many records but you only wish to view some of them. Data can be analysed by applying multiple filters, allowing various combinations of data to be analysed.

Illustration 4: Applying a filter to data

(1) Open the 'Stockman Ltd' spreadsheet.

(2) Let's say we just want to find inventory records relating to suppliers B and C.

(3) Select **Filter** from the **Sort & Filter** drop-down menu.

(4) Click on the drop-down arrow that has appeared at the top of the Supplier column.

(5) Deselect (ie click on the box to remove the tick) **Select All**, then select B and C.

(6) Click on **OK**.

Only the records relating to suppliers B and C are visible and these can be manipulated (eg sorted) as an independent subset of the whole table.

Note that the other records are still there and are included in the total value figure. It's simply that they have been hidden for presentation.

You will also see a little funnel symbol at the top of the Supplier column; this informs you that there is filtering in place.

Make all the records visible again by removing the filter:

(1) Drop-down arrow in the Supplier column.
(2) Select **Select All**.
(3) Click on **OK**.
(4) Sort the data back into Part code order if it's not already in that order.

To get rid of the little filter arrows, click on the funnel symbol in the **Sort & Filter** area of the Ribbon to disengage it.

Find and replace

Let's now say that Supplier A Ltd has been taken over and that its name has changed to Acorn plc.

Illustration 5: Using find and replace

(1) Make all the records visible again by removing the filter, if you haven't already
(2) Click on the **Find & Select** symbol and select **Find** (or press **Ctrl + F**)
(3) Enter A Ltd in the **Find what**: box
(4) Click on the **Replace** tab and enter Acorn Plc in the **Replace with**: box
(5) Click on **Replace All**

Note. You could instead click on **Find & Select>Replace** (or press **Ctrl + H**) as a shortcut.

You should see that all occurrences of 'A Ltd' have been replaced by 'Acorn plc'.

If no range is specified before this step then the whole spreadsheet would be affected. If a range is specified, the search and replace occurs only within that range.

BPP
LEARNING MEDIA

Concatenate

The concatenate function is used to combine two text cells into a single cell.

This is done by using the formula =CONCATENATE(text1, [text 2]…)

C1	▾ :	×	✓	fx	=CONCATENATE(A1,B1)		
	A	B	C	D	E	F	G	H
1	Spread	sheet	Spreadsheet					
2								
3								

If the formula is used as shown above, the words will be joined together with no space between.

If a space is to be included between the words, this can be achieved by using quotation marks around a single space between the two text references in the formula.

=CONCATENATE(text1, " ",[text 2]…)

E1	▾ :	×	✓	fx	=CONCATENATE(C1," ",D1)		
	A	B	C	D	E	F	G	H
1	Spread	sheet	Spreadsheet	skills	Spreadsheet skills			
2								
3								
4								

This is particularly useful when joining data such as first name and last name.

Removing duplicates

If you wish to remove duplicate data from a worksheet this can be achieved by selecting the required data then **Data>Remove Duplicates**. From here you can choose the columns to show the number of duplicate and unique data contained.

2.1 Pivot tables

Pivot tables are a very powerful way of analysing data. Look at the following simple example relating to sales by a music company.

	A	B	C
1	**Sales data**		
2			
3	**Customer**	**Source**	**Amount spent (£)**
4	Bill	CDs	50
5	Chris	Vinyl	10
6	Sandra	Merchandise	30
7	Graham	CDs	45
8	Chris	Merchandise	20
9	Chris	Vinyl	10
10	Chris	CDs	10
11	Caroline	Merchandise	30
12	Graham	Tickets	75
13	Fred	Vinyl	30
14	Bill	CDs	20
15	Graham	CDs	60
16	Chris	Vinyl	10
17	Sandra	Tickets	50
18	Bill	Tickets	26
19	Caroline	Vinyl	24
20			
21		Total	£500

BPP
LEARNING MEDIA

The information has simply been listed and totalled on the spreadsheet. It would be useful to be able to show:

- Sales per customer
- Sales by source

Ideally, we would like to produce a table which displays sales by both source and by customer: this type of table is called a **pivot table**.

Illustration 6: Creating a pivot table

(1) Open the spreadsheet file called 'Pivot Table Example' which contains the above data.

(2) Select the range A4:C19.

(3) On the Ribbon, select **Insert>PivotTable.**

(4) Select the **Existing Worksheet** radio button on the **Create PivotTable** option window.

(5) Enter E4 as the location.

(6) Click **OK**. The **PivotTable Field List** window opens.

(7) Check Customer, Source, Amount spent (£).

(8) You will see that Customer and Source go by default into **Row Labels**. The resulting table is quite useful, but not quite what we wanted.

Therefore:

(9) Drag Customer from **Row Labels** to **Column Labels**.

The pivot table is now transformed into the two-dimensional table we want.

(10) Tidy it up a little by selecting F5 to L5 and right-justifying these names by clicking on the appropriate **Home>Alignment** button on the Ribbon.

Note the two drop-down arrows on the pivot table that allow filtering of the data.

Sum of Amount spent (£)	Column Labels ▼						
Row Labels ▼	Bill	Caroline	Chris	Fred	Graham	Sandra	Grand Total
CDs	70		10		105		185
Merchandise		30	20			30	80
Tickets	26				75	50	151
Vinyl		24	30	30			84
Grand Total	96	54	60	30	180	80	500

If you had difficulty with this, the spreadsheet called 'Pivot Table Result Excel 2013' is available within the downloaded files.

Experiment with different settings. Clicking on the pivot table will bring up the **PivotTable Field List** window again if it has disappeared.

Note that if the original data is altered, the pivot table does **not** change until you right-click on it and select **Refresh** from the list of options.

Pivot charts

The information contained in a pivot table can be visually presented using a pivot chart.

---

(1) Click on any cell inside the pivot table.

(2) On the **Insert** tab, click **Pivot chart** and select one of the graph types. For example, 'clustered column'

Note. Any changes you make to the pivot table will be immediately reflected in the pivot chart and vice versa.

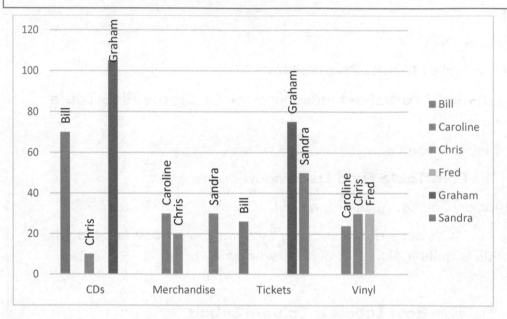

2.2 Sharing workbooks

It is possible to share a workbook with colleagues so that the same file can be viewed by more than one person at a time. This can be done in a number of ways.

Send as an attachment

One way to share a spreadsheet with colleagues is to send it as an attachment in an email. If your computer is set up with a mail client such as Microsoft Outlook you can click **File Button>Save & Send>Send Using Email** to quickly send the spreadsheet you are working on as an attachment.

Alternatively, you can first draft the email and attach the spreadsheet using your email program's options and the Windows Explorer menu.

However, if each recipient of the email makes changes to the document, this will lead to the existence of a number of different versions of the same document, and a potential loss of version control. This is not, therefore, a recommended method of sharing spreadsheets.

Save to a shared network server

Another way to make a spreadsheet available to colleagues is to save it in a place on the network server that is also accessible to them. Anyone with access to that particular location will be able to open the file – but if more than one person tries to open the file, only the first person will be able to make changes to it. Anyone else subsequently opening the file will only be able to open a 'Read Only' version of it, so they will be able to view the contents but not make any changes.

This method prevents loss of version control, but is not particularly useful if other people wish to make changes at the same time.

Share workbook method

A more practical method is to use the inbuilt sharing function in Excel. This allows different people to open and make changes to the same document at the same time, and for these changes to be tracked.

Click the **Review** tab on the Ribbon. In the **Changes** section click the **Share Workbook** button. Click the **Editing** tab and select **Allow changes by more than one user at the same time**. From this tab you can also see who has the document open.

Other settings are available from the **Advanced** tab, such as choosing how long to keep the change history for, how frequently to update changes and what to do if users make conflicting changes.

To stop any tracked changes from being lost click **Protect and Share Workbook** and click **Sharing with tracked changes**. This option also allows you to set a password so only those with the password can make changes.

3 Three-dimensional (multi-sheet) spreadsheets

3.1 Background

In early spreadsheet packages, a spreadsheet file consisted of a single worksheet. As mentioned earlier, Excel provides the option of multi-sheet spreadsheets, consisting of a series of related sheets.

For example, suppose you were producing a profit forecast for two regions, and a combined forecast for the total of the regions. This situation would be suited to using separate worksheets for each region and another for the total. This approach is sometimes referred to as working in **three dimensions**, as you are able to flip between different sheets stacked in front of, or behind, each other. Cells in one sheet may **refer** to cells in another sheet. So, in our example, the formulas in the cells in the total sheet would refer to the cells in the other sheets.

Excel has a series of 'tabs', one for each worksheet, at the bottom of the spreadsheet.

3.2 How many worksheets?

Excel can be set up so that it always opens a fresh file with a certain number of worksheets ready and waiting for you. Click on **Office button>Excel Options>Popular**, and set the number **Include this many sheets** option to the number you would like each new workbook to contain (sheets may be added or deleted later).

If you subsequently want to insert more sheets you just click on the new sheet tab.

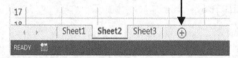

By default, sheets are called Sheet 1, Sheet 2 etc. However, these may be changed. To rename a sheet in Excel, right-click on its index tab and choose the **Rename** option. You can drag the sheets into a different order by clicking on the tab, holding down the mouse button and dragging a sheet to its new position. Index tabs can also be formatted in a variety of colours by right-click on its index tab and selecting the **Tab Color** option.

3.3 Pasting from one sheet to another

When building a spreadsheet that will contain a number of worksheets with identical structure, users often set up one sheet, then copy that sheet and amend its contents.

To copy a worksheet in Excel, from within the worksheet you wish to copy, select **Home>Cells>Format>Move or Copy Sheet** (or right-click the worksheet tab and select **Move or Copy Sheet**) and tick the **Create a copy** box.

A 'Total' sheet would use the same structure, but would contain formulas totalling the individual sheets.

Illustration 7: Linking worksheets

The following illustration shows how to link worksheets with formulas.

Formulas on one sheet may refer to data held on another sheet. The links within such a formula may be established using the following steps.

Step 1   In the cell that you want to refer to a cell from another sheet, type =.

Step 2   Click on the index tab for the sheet containing the cell you want to refer to and select the cell in question.

Step 3   Press **Enter**.

(1) Open the spreadsheet called '3D spreadsheet example'.

    This consists of three worksheets. The Branch A and Branch B sheets hold simple trading accounts and income statements. There are both numbers and formulas in those sheets. The Company sheet contains only headings, but is set out in the same pattern as the two branch sheets.

    We want to combine the Branch figures onto the Company sheet.

(2) On the Company sheet, make D2 the active cell.

(3) Enter **=**

(4) Click on Branch A and click on D2.

(5) Enter **+**

(6) Click on Branch B and click on D2.

(7) Press **Enter**.

    You will see that the formula ='Branch A'!D2+'Branch B'!D2 is now in cell D2 of the Company sheet and that the number displayed is 500,000, the sum of the sales in each branch.

    In the Company sheet, copy D2 (**Ctrl+C**) and paste (**Ctrl+V**) to D3, D4, C6, C7, D8, and D9 to complete the income statement.

The company sheet will now look like this:

▲	A	B	C	D
1	**Company**		£	£
2	Sales			500,000
3	Cost of sales			270,000
4	Gross profit			230,000
5	Expenses:			
6	Selling and distribution		70,000	
7	Administration		45,000	
8				115,000
9	Profit for the period			115,000
10				
11				

This is arithmetically correct, but needs lines to format it correctly.

Use the border facility in **Home>Font** to insert appropriate single and double lines (**borders**) in the cells:

The final consolidated results should look like:

	A	B	C	D
1	**Company**		£	£
2	Sales			500,000
3	Cost of sales			270,000
4	Gross profit			230,000
5	Expenses:			
6	Selling and distribution		70,000	
7	Administration		45,000	
8				115,000
9	Profit for the period			115,000

Note that if you change any figures in Branch A or Branch B, the figures will also change on the Company spreadsheet.

Files and documents (eg spreadsheets and Word documents) can also be **direct referenced** and linked by using **Paste Special>Paste Link**. To check the status of any links created go to **Data>Edit Links** and this will show a list of links their source and options to update and break links.

3.4 Uses for multi-sheet spreadsheets

There are a wide range of situations suited to the multi-sheet approach. A variety of possible uses follow.

(a)   A spreadsheet could use one sheet for variables, a second for calculations, and a third for outputs.

(b)   To enable quick and easy **consolidation** of similar sets of data, for example the financial results of two subsidiaries or the budgets of two departments.

(c)   To provide different views of the same data. For instance, you could have one sheet of data sorted into product code order and another sorted into product name order.

3.5 Formatting data as a table

You can format data within a spreadsheet as a table. This provides you with another way to present and manipulate data.

Creating a table

First we will create a table and then we'll look at what we can do with it.

Illustration 8: Formatting a table

(1)   **Open** the 'Tables example' spreadsheet from the downloaded files. This uses almost the same data as in the previous exercise, so should look familiar to you.

(2)   Select the cells that contain the data (A3 to G15).

(3)   On the **Home** tab of the Ribbon select **Format as Table** from the **Styles** section.

(4)   A gallery of styles will appear, so choose one of the formats (any one will do). Check that the correct data for the table is selected in the white box and tick the box **My table has headers**.

(5)   Click **OK**.

---

(6) Your table should now look something like this, depending on which format you chose:

	A	B	C	D	E	F	G
1	Stockman Ltd						
2							
3	Part cod ▾	Supplie ▾	Quantit ▾	Reorder leve ▾	Unit pric ▾	Value ▾	Order neede ▾
4	129394	A Ltd	124	100	20	2,480.00	
5	129395	B Ltd	4325	4500	14	60,550.00	Yes
6	129396	F Ltd	4626	4000	12	55,512.00	
7	129397	A Ltd	583	500	14	8,162.00	
8	129398	D Ltd	43	50	37	1,591.00	Yes
9	129399	E Ltd	837	1000	65	54,405.00	Yes
10	129400	B Ltd	84	50	34	2,856.00	
11	129401	F Ltd	4847	5000	20	96,940.00	Yes
12	129402	D Ltd	4632	4000	10	46,320.00	
13	129403	A Ltd	41	40	34	1,394.00	
14	129404	E Ltd	5578	5000	25	139,450.00	
15	129405	C Ltd	5	10	35	175.00	Yes

You will notice that there are **Sort & Filter** drop-down arrows at the top of each column in the header row. This is just one of the benefits of formatting data as a table: automatic **Sort & Filter**.

Other benefits of formatting data as a table

Other benefits include:

(a) **Easy row and column selection**

Move the cursor to the top of the header row of the table and it will change to a thick pointing arrow. When you click, just the data in that column will be selected (and not the empty cells below the data). You can select data rows in a similar way.

The whole table can be selected by hovering near the table's top-left corner, until the arrow becomes thick and starts pointing towards the bottom right-hand corner.

(b) **Visible header row when scrolling**

When you scroll down past the bottom of the table the column letters become the table's column names, so long as you have clicked anywhere inside the table before starting to scroll.

3	Part cod ▾	Supplie ▾	Quantit ▾	Reorder leve ▾	Unit pric ▾	Value ▾	Order neede ▾
4	129394	A Ltd	124	100	20	2,480.00	
5	129395	B Ltd	4325	4500	14	60,550.00	Yes
6	129396	F Ltd	4626	4000	12	55,512.00	
7	129397	A Ltd	583	500	14	8,162.00	
8	129398	D Ltd	43	50	37	1,591.00	Yes
9	129399	E Ltd	837	1000	65	54,405.00	Yes
10	129400	B Ltd	84	50	34	2,856.00	
11	129401	F Ltd	4847	5000	20	96,940.00	Yes
12	129402	D Ltd	4632	4000	10	46,320.00	
13	129403	A Ltd	41	40	34	1,394.00	
14	129404	E Ltd	5578	5000	25	139,450.00	
15	129405	C Ltd	5	10	35	175.00	Yes
16							

(c) **Automatic table expansion**

Type anything into any of the cells around the table and the table will automatically grow to include your new data. The formatting of the table will automatically adjust (this will also happen if you insert or delete a row or column).

4: More advanced spreadsheet techniques (Excel 2013)

(d)   **Automatic formula copying**

If you enter a formula in a cell around the table and click **Enter**, the column will automatically resize to fit the formula, which is automatically copied down to fill the entire column alongside your data.

Changing the design of the table

You can change how the table looks by clicking anywhere in the table and selecting the **Design** tab from the **Table Tools** toolbar.

From here there are a number of **Table Style Options** that you can play around with, such as formatting a **First Column** or **Last Column**, adding a **Total Row** and changing the **Table Style**.

You can also choose to give your table a name, so that any formula you enter which uses the figures from the table will refer to that table by its name.

So, for example, type 'Parts' into the **Table Name** box:

Now any formula entered in the column next to the table will refer to the table by name. Try it!

f_x	=Parts([@Quantity])*Parts([@[Unit price]])									
C	D	E	F	G	H	I	J	K	L

Quantity	Reorder level	Unit price	Value	Order needed	Column				
124	100	20	2,480.00		2480				
4325	4500	14	60,550.00	Yes	60550	=Parts([@Quantity])*Parts([@[Unit price]])			
4626	4000	12	55,512.00		55512				
583	500	14	8,162.00		8162				
43	50	37	1,591.00	Yes	1591				
837	1000	65	54,405.00	Yes	54405				

Table tools

From the **Design** tab you can also:

- Choose to **Remove Duplicates**, which, as the name suggests, removes duplicate data from the table. This technique will help ensure data has been entered accurately.

- Remove the table formatting completely by selecting **Convert to Range**. You may then wish to clear the formatting. You can easily do this by clicking **Clear** on the **Editing** section of the **Home** tab and choosing **Clear formats**.

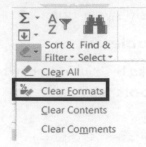

3.6 Look-up tables

The Look-up function allows you to find and use data that is held in a table.

VLOOKUP is used for finding data in **v**ertical columns.

HLOOKUP is used for finding data in **h**orizontal rows.

Here is a simple example:

	A	B	C	D	E	F	G	H	I
1	**Salesman Ltd**								
2	**Part code**	**VATcode**	**Unit price**		VAT rate	20.0%			
3			£						
4	129394	1	20.00						
5	129395	1	14.00		**Invoice**				
6	129396	0	12.00						
7	129397	0	14.00						
8	129398	1	37.00		Part code	Quantity	Unit price	VAT	£
9	129399	0	65.00		129396	10	12.00	0	120.00
10	129400	1	34.00					Net	120.00
11	129401	0	20.00					VAT	0.00
12	129402	1	10.00					Total	120.00
13	129403	0	34.00						
14	129404	0	25.00						
15	129405	1	35.00						
16									
17									

On the left is a price list. If a part has a VAT code of 1, then VAT will be charged at the rate as set in cell F2; if the VAT code is 0, then no VAT is chargeable.

To create this invoice, you would look down the part numbers column until you found 129396. You would then read across to find the unit price and VAT code and, together with the quantity sold, you could create the invoice.

This process has been automated in the spreadsheet 'Salesman Ltd'.

(1) Open the spreadsheet called 'Salesman Ltd'.
(2) Click on cell G9 to reveal the use of the VLOOKUP function.

Cell G9 holds the formula =VLOOKUP(E9,A4:C15,3, FALSE)

This means: look for the value held in cell E9, in the first row of the range A4:C15, and return the value in the third column of the range: it will return the price relating to the part number. **FALSE** (at the end of the statement) asks it to find an exact match so if a non-existent part code is entered in E9 you will get an error message (**#N/A**).

Similarly, cell H9 holds the formula =VLOOKUP(E9,A4:C15,2) and will return the VAT code relating to the part number.

Cell I11 holds a conditional (IF) function that will calculate VAT if the VAT code is 1 and insert 0 if the VAT code is 0.

Note that some cells have been formatted to show two decimal places and some to show no decimal places. Cell F2 is formatted as a percentage and, because VAT might need to be changed, VAT is held in only one location with other cells referring to it.

Try out different part codes and quantities in the invoice.

3.7 Importing data to Excel

You may wish to include data in a spreadsheet from, say, a Microsoft Word document, a PowerPoint presentation or another spreadsheet.

The easiest way to do this is select the text you wish to include, click the **Home** tab and click **Copy** (or press **Ctrl + C**).

Open the spreadsheet that you wish to use the data in (if it is not already open) and click the **Paste** button (or press **Ctrl + V**).

Assessment focus point

Ensure you understand, and can practice using, the main data manipulation tools in this section. Practising using the different data tools will build understanding of what information is produced and any limitations.

---

4 Changes in assumptions (what-if? analysis)

In Chapter 3 we referred to the need to design a spreadsheet so that **changes in assumptions** do **not** require **major changes** to the spreadsheet. In our 'Costing exercise' workbook we set up two separate areas of the spreadsheet, one for assumptions and opening balances, and one for the calculations and results. We could simply change the values in the assumptions cells to see how any changes in assumptions affect the results.

However, if we have more than one value to change, or we want to see the result of a number of different assumption changes, we can use one of the three 'What-if' functions.

4.1 Data tables

A **data table** is a way to see different results by altering an input cell in a formula. You can create one- or two-variable data tables.

Let's try creating a one-variable data table.

---

(1) Open the spreadsheet called 'Mortgage'.

(2) Enter 1% to 10% in cells E8 to N8 as shown below.

	A	B	C	D	E	F	G	H	I	J	K	L	M	N
1	Assumptions													
2														
3	Annual interest rate		10%											
4	Amount of loan (£)		20,000											
5	Period of loan		20 years											
6														
7	Calculation of monthly repayments over a reducing balance mortgage lasting (years)									20				
8					1%	2%	3%	4%	5%	6%	7%	8%	9%	10%
9	Monthly repayment			-£193.00										
10														

(3) Select cells D8 to N9.

(4) **Click Data>What-If Analysis>Data Table**.

(5) Here you want your data table to fill in the values in row 9, based on the results if the value in cell C3 were to change to a different percentage, so choose the **Row input cell** box and enter C3.

You should get the following results:

	1%	2%	3%	4%	5%	6%	7%	8%	9%	10%
-£193.00	-91.9789	-101.177	-110.92	-121.196	-131.991	-143.286	-155.06	-167.288	-179.945	-193.004

The table would look better if the numbers were formatted in the same way as the first result in cell D9. An easy way to copy a format from one cell to another is to click on the cell whose format you wish to copy, then click the **Format Painter** button on the **Clipboard** area of the **Home** tab and then click on the cells you wish to format.

Try it now. Click on cell D9, then click the **Format Painter** button. Now select cells E9:N9. You should see:

	1%	2%	3%	4%	5%	6%	7%	8%	9%	10%
-£193.00	-£91.98	-£101.18	-£110.92	-£121.20	-£131.99	-£143.29	-£155.06	-£167.29	-£179.95	-£193.00

Note. If you double-click the **Format Painter** button you can then click any number of cells afterwards to apply that same format. To stop the **Format Painter**, simply click **Esc** (Escape).

Now let's try a two-variable data table, using the same workbook. This time we want to see the result if both the interest rate and the number of years of the loan change.

(1) Rename the worksheet you have been working on to 'One variable'. Now select Sheet 2 (or insert a new worksheet if necessary) and rename it 'Two variable'. This is the sheet that we will now use.

(2) **Copy** the data on the 'One variable' worksheet (**Ctrl + C**) and paste (**Ctrl + V**) into the new worksheet.

(3) Select cells E8 to N8 and move them down by one cell (ie to E9 to N9). You can do this by hovering over the selected cells until a cross with four arrow heads appears, then click and drag to cell E9. Alternatively, **Cut** (**Ctrl + X**) and then **Paste** (**Ctrl + V**) to cell E9.

(4) In cells D10 to D14 insert different loan periods. We have used 10, 15, 20, 25 and 30 years, as shown below:

-£193.00	1%	2%	3%	4%	5%	6%	7%	8%	9%	10%
10										
15										
20										
25										
30										

(5) Select cells D9 to N14.

(6) Click **Data>What-If Analysis>Data Table**.

(7) Here you want the data table to fill in the values based on the results if the value in cell C3 were to change to a different percentage (as shown in row 9) and also if the loan period in C5 changes (as shown in column D). So, choose the **Row input cell** box and enter C3 and then select the **Column input cell** box and enter C5.

You should get the following results:

-£193.00	1%	2%	3%	4%	5%	6%	7%	8%	9%	10%
10	-£175.21	-£184.03	-£193.12	-£202.49	-£212.13	-£222.04	-£232.22	-£242.66	-£253.35	-£264.30
15	-£119.70	-£128.70	-£138.12	-£147.94	-£158.16	-£168.77	-£179.77	-£191.13	-£202.85	-£214.92
20	-£91.98	-£101.18	-£110.92	-£121.20	-£131.99	-£143.29	-£155.06	-£167.29	-£179.95	-£193.00
25	-£75.37	-£84.77	-£94.84	-£105.57	-£116.92	-£128.86	-£141.36	-£154.36	-£167.84	-£181.74
30	-£64.33	-£73.92	-£84.32	-£95.48	-£107.36	-£119.91	-£133.06	-£146.75	-£160.92	-£175.51

Format cells E10 to N14 in the same way as cell D9.

Finally practise saving the file as 'Mortgage – Data tables' in a new folder on your computer using **File button>Save as**. Choose an appropriate name for the folder – it's your choice!

4.2 Scenarios

The **Scenarios** function allows you to change information in cells that affect the final totals of a formula and to prepare instant reports showing the results of all scenarios together.

Using the spreadsheet 'Costing Exercise – Finished', we will show the result of changing the following assumptions:

(a) The chargeout rate for the Accounting Technician is now £30.00.

(b) The cost of a laptop has increased to £115.00 per week.

(c) The increase in chargeout rate for the secretary has been altered to 8%.

You could simply change the relevant cells in the spreadsheet to reflect these changes in assumptions. However, we are going to use the Scenario Manager function.

Illustration 9: Using the scenarios function

(1) Select the **Data** tab and, from the **Data Tools** section, click **What-If Analysis>Scenario Manager**.

(2) Click **Add** and give the scenario an appropriate name, for example 'Original costing exercise'.

(3) Press the tab button or click in the **Changing cells** box and, based on the information we used above, select the cells with the changing data, ignoring the change to the opening bank balance. To select cells that are not next to each other, use the **Ctrl** button. You should **Ctrl-click** on cells B4, B6, B7.

(4) Click **OK**.

(5) You are now asked for **Scenario Values**. This will show the values currently in the cells specified, which are our original figures, so click **OK**.

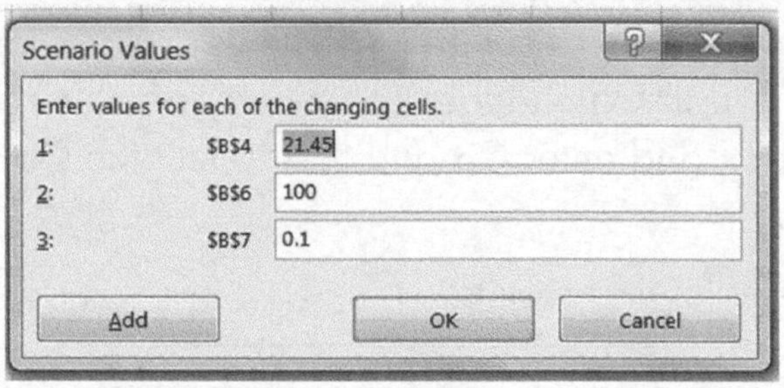

(6) We now need to enter our new values. Click **Add** and type a new **Name** (for example 'Costing exercise 2'). The **Changing Cells** box will already contain the correct cells.

(7) Click **OK**.

(8) In the **Scenario Values** boxes change the values as follows, and click **OK**.

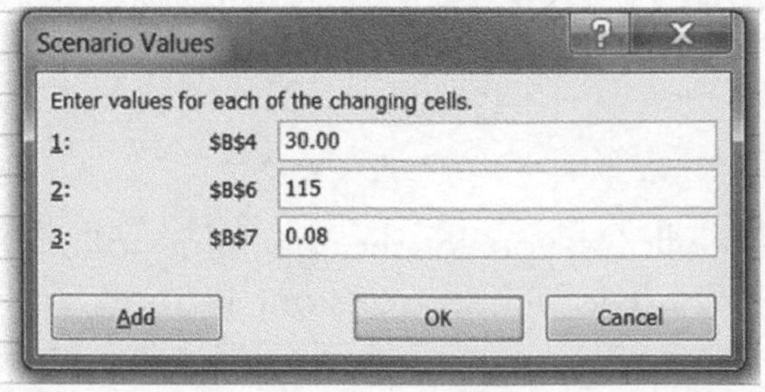

---

(9) Your second scenario should be highlighted. Now if you click on **Show**, the figures in your assumptions table should automatically change and you can view the results.

	A	B	C	D	E	F	G
	L27						
1	Internal chargeout rates						
2	Divisional chief accountant	£72.50					
3	Assistant accountant	£38.00					
4	Accounting technician	£30.00					
5	Secretary	£17.30					
6	Laptop cost	£115.00					
7	Chargeout rate	8%					
8							
9	Costs	Week 1	Week 2	Week 3	Week 4	Total	
10	Divisional chief accountant	£0.00	£326.25	£489.38	£435.00	£1,250.63	
11	Assistant accountant	£760.00	£1,520.00	£1,330.00	£0.00	£3,610.00	
12	Accounting technician	£960.00	£1,200.00	£1,125.00	£0.00	£3,285.00	
13	Secretary	£259.50	£557.93	£695.98	£0.00	£1,513.40	
14	laptops	£230.00	£230.00	£230.00		£690.00	
15	Total	£1,979.50	£3,604.18	£3,640.35	£435.00	£10,349.03	
16							
17	Hours	Week 1	Week 2	Week 3	Week 4	Total	
18	Divisional chief accountant	0	4.5	6.75	6	17.25	
19	Assistant accountant	20	40	35		95	
20	Accounting technician	32	40	37.5		109.5	
21	Secretary	15	32.25	37.25		84.5	
22	Total	67	116.75	116.5	6	306.25	
23							
24	Laptops	2	2	2			
25							
26							

(10) Click back on your original 'Costing exercise' and then click **Show** and the numbers will change back.

Note. You may need to make your screen smaller to view the whole sheet at the same time. You can do this by clicking **View** on the Ribbon, then in the **Zoom** section clicking on **Zoom** and choosing a smaller percentage. 75% should be perfect.

You can also easily and quickly create a report from the scenarios.

(1) Click **Data>What-If Analysis>Scenario Manager**.

(2) Click the **Summary** button.

(3) In the **Result cells** box choose the cells to go into the report, ie the ones you want to see the results of. As we are interested in the final cost select cell F15. This creates a separate **Scenario Summary** worksheet. Open the 'Costing Exercise – What-if' spreadsheet if you do not see the following report.

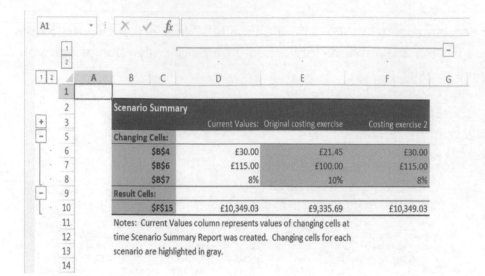

4.3 Goal seek

What if you already know the result you want from a formula but not the value the formula itself needs to calculate the result? In this case you should use the **Goal Seek** function, which is located in the **Data Tools** section of the **Data** tab on the Ribbon.

Open the original 'Mortgage' spreadsheet from the downloaded files. Let's assume that we have enough income to make a monthly mortgage payment of £300 and want to know how many years it will take to pay off the mortgage.

(1) Copy the data on Sheet 1 and paste it to Sheet 2.

(2) Click **Data>What-If Analysis>Goal Seek**.

(3) Enter $D$9 at **Set cell**, as this is the figure we know and enter -300 in the **To value** box (make sure that you enter a negative figure to match the figure already in D9).

(4) Enter $C$5 in the **By changing cell** box, as this is the figure we are looking for.

(5) Click **OK**.

BPP
LEARNING MEDIA

Goal seek will find the solution, 8.14 years, and insert it in cell C5.

	A	B	C	D	E	F	G	H	I	J	K	L	M	N	O
1	Assumptions														
2															
3	Annual interest rate		10%												
4	Amount of loan (£)		20,000												
5	Period of loan		8.143044	years											
6															
7	Calculation of monthly repayments over a reducing balance mortgage lasting (years)								8.1						
8															
9	Monthly repayment		-£300.00												
10															
11															
12															
13															
14															

Goal Seek Status

Goal Seeking with Cell D9 found a solution.

Target value: -300
Current value: -£300.00

[Step] [Pause] [OK] [Cancel]

Assessment focus point

In the exam, you may be asked to use one or more of these forecasting tools, such as **Goal Seek**. It is essential that you have a full understanding of what each tool may be used for and how it can answer the exam question. Read the question carefully to ensure the tool you select answers the question in the most appropriate manner.

5 Statistical functions

Assessment focus point

It is unlikely that you will be tested on statistical functions such as preparing trends, moving averages and histograms. The following information is provided to develop your spreadsheet skills further in these areas. If you wish, you may skip section 5 and move directly to section 6.

5.1 Linear regression, trends and forecasts

Excel contains powerful statistical tools for the analysis of information, such as how costs vary with production volumes and how sales vary through the year.

Look at the following example of costs and volume:

Month	Volume Units	Costs £
1	1,000	8,500
2	1,200	9,600
3	1,800	14,000

Month	Volume Units	Costs £
4	900	7,000
5	2,000	16,000
6	400	5,000

It is clear that at higher production volumes costs are higher, but it would be useful to find a relationship between these variables so that we could predict what costs might be if production were forecast at, say, 1,500 units.

The first investigation we could perform is simply to draw a graph of costs against volume. Volume is the independent variable (it causes the costs) so should run on the horizontal (x) axis.

Illustration 10: Trend lines

Open the spreadsheet called 'Cost_volume' and draw a scatter graph showing cost against volume, with appropriate labels and legends.

(1) Select the range B1:C7.

(2) Using **Insert/Charts** from the Ribbon, choose the top left Scatter graph type).

It should look something like the following:

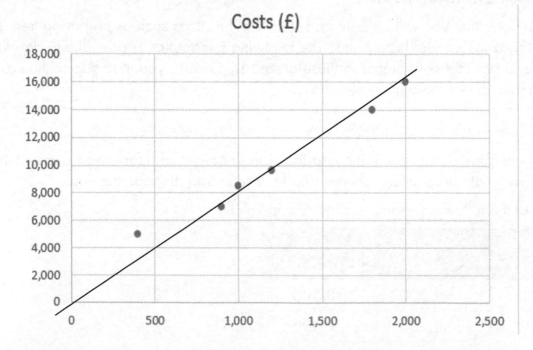

Costs (£)

The straight line through the points has been manually drawn here to show that there's clearly a good association between volume and cost, because the points do not miss the line by much; but we want to analyse this properly, so that we can make a fairly good prediction of costs at output of, say, 1,500 units.

Lines of the sort above have a general equation of the type:

y = **mx + b**

Here **y** = Total costs

    x = Volume

    m = Variable cost per unit (the slope of the line)

    b = The fixed cost (where the line crosses the y axis: the cost even at zero volume)

Excel provides two easy ways of finding the figures we need for predicting values.

Find the trend:

(1) On the same 'Cost_volume' spreadsheet, enter 1,500 in cell B9.

(2) Now click on cell C9.

(3) From the Ribbon choose **Formulas>More Functions>Statistical**.

FILE	HOME	INSERT	PAGE LAYOUT	FORMULAS	DAT

fx Insert Function

Σ AutoSum ▾   Logical ▾   Lookup & Reference
Recently Used ▾   Text ▾   Math & Trig ▾
Financial ▾   Date & Time ▾   More Functions ▾

Function Library

More Functions menu:
- Statistical ▶
- Engineering ▶
- Cube ▶
- Information ▶
- Compatibility ▶
- Web ▶

C9

	A	B	C	D
1	**Month**	**Volume**	**Costs (£)**	
2	1	1,000	8,500	
3	2	1,200	9,600	
4	3	1,800	14,000	
5	4	900	7,000	
6	5	2,000	16,000	
7	6	400	5,000	
8				
9				
10				

(4) Scroll down the list until you get to **TREND** and choose that.

(5) For **Known_y's** select the range C2:C7.

(6) For **Known_x's** select the range B2:B7.

(These ranges are the raw material which the calculation uses)

For **New_x's**, enter B9, the volume for which we want the costs to be predicted.

The number 12,003 should appear in cell C9. That is the predicted cost for output of 1,500 units – in line with the graph. In practice, we would use 12,000. Altering the value in B9 will produce the corresponding predicted cost.

A second way of analysing this data will allow us to find the variable and fixed costs of the units (**m** and **b** in the equation **y = mx +b**).

(1) To find **m**, use the statistical function **LINEST** and assign the **Known_y's** and **Known_x's** as before. You should get the answer 7.01, the variable cost per unit.

(2) To find the intersection, **b**, use the statistical function **INTERCEPT**. You should get the answer 1,486.

Note. These can be used to predict the costs of 1,500 units by saying:

Total costs = 1,486 + 7.01 × 1,500 = 12,001, more or less as before.

The spreadsheet called 'Cost_volume finished' contains the graph, and the three statistical functions just described.

5.2 Moving averages

AAT only require knowledge of the area of moving averages, but it is important to understand what we mean by moving averages and how they can be calculated. Note that you will not be asked to reproduce this in the live assessment, however you need to understand what it is and how it works.

Look at this data

Year	Quarter	Time series	Sales £000
20X6	1	1	989.0
	2	2	990.0
	3	3	994.0
	4	4	1,015.0
20X7	1	5	1,030.0
	2	6	1,042.5
	3	7	1,036.0
	4	8	1,056.5
20X8	1	9	1,071.0
	2	10	1,083.5
	3	11	1,079.5
	4	12	1,099.5

Year	Quarter	Time series	Sales £000
20X9	1	13	1,115.5
	2	14	1,127.5
	3	15	1,123.5
	4	16	1,135.0
20Y0	1	17	1,140.0

You might be able to see that the data follows a seasonal pattern: for example there always seems to be a dip in Quarter 3 and a peak in Quarter 2. It is more obvious if plotted as a time series of sales against the consecutively numbered quarters.

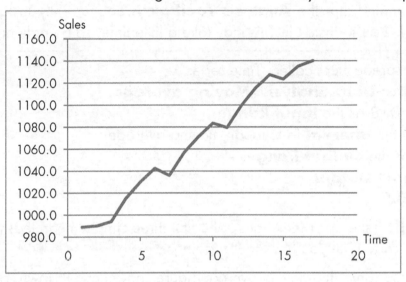

The **moving average** technique attempts to even out the seasonal variations. Here, because we seem to have data repeating every four readings, a four-part moving average would be appropriate. If you were trading five days a week and wanted to even out the sales, a five-part moving average would be suitable.

The moving average is calculated as follows:

Take the first four figures and average them:

$$\frac{(989.0+990.0+994.0+1,015.0)}{4} = 997.0$$

Then move on one season:

$$\frac{(990.0+994.0+1,015.0+1,030.0)}{4} = 1,007.3$$

and so on, always averaging out all four seasons. Each average will include a high season and a low season.

That's rather tedious to do manually and Excel provides a function to do it automatically. To access this analysis function you must have the **Excel Analysis**

ToolPak installed. If it is installed there will be an **Analysis>Data Analysis** tab in the **Data** section of the Ribbon.

If it is not already installed, you can install it as follows:

(1) Click the **File Button**, and then click **Excel Options**.

(2) Click **Add-Ins** and then, from the **Manage** box, select **Excel Add-Ins**.

(3) Click **Go**.

(4) In the **Add-Ins available** box, select the **Analysis ToolPak** checkbox, and then click **OK**.

Tip. If **Analysis ToolPak** is not listed in the **Add-Ins available** box, click **Browse** to locate it.

If you are prompted that the **Analysis ToolPak** is not currently installed on your computer, click **Yes** to install it. This may take a little time, so be patient!

(1) Open the spreadsheet called 'Time series'.

(2) Select **Data>Data analysis>Moving average**.

(3) Select D2:D18 as the **Input Range**.

(4) Enter 4 as the **Interval** (a four-part moving average).

(5) Enter F2 as the **Output Range**.

(6) Check **Chart Output**.

(7) Click on **OK**.

Don't worry about the error messages – the first three simply mean that you can't do a four-part average until you have four readings.

Move your cursor onto the moving average figures and move it down, one cell at a time, to see how the averages move.

Notice on the graph how the Forecast line (the moving average) is much smoother than the Actual figures. This makes predicting future sales much easier.

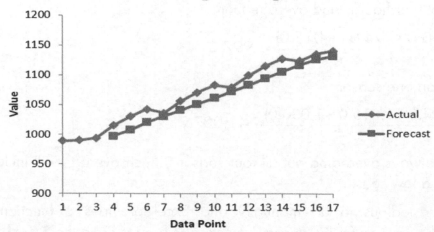

5.3 Mean, mode and median

These are three measures of what is known as the 'location' of data – they give an indication of whereabouts the data is clustered.

Mean (or arithmetic mean) is the ordinary average (add up the readings and divide by the number of readings).

Mode is the most frequently occurring item. For example, in a shoe shop, the arithmetic mean of shoe sizes is not much use. The shopkeeper is more interested in the most common shoe size.

Median is the value of the middle item if they are arranged in ascending or descending sequence. As well as medians you can have 'quartiles' (upper and lower) dividing the population into top one-quarter, lowest three-quarters (or *vice versa*) and 'deciles' (10:90 splits).

Excel allows all of these measures to be calculated (or identified) easily.

---

(1) Open the spreadsheet called 'Student Results'.

This lists the exam results of 23 students. They are currently displayed in alphabetical order. Don't worry about the column headed 'Bins' for now.

Enter 'Mean' in cell A28, then make cell B28 active.

(2) Choose **Formulas>Σ AutoSum>Average** and accept the range offered. 58.56 is the arithmetic mean of the marks.

(3) Enter 'Median' in cell A29, then make cell B29 active.

(4) Choose **Formulas>More Functions>Statistical>MEDIAN**.

(5) Enter the range B4:B26 for **Number 1**.

You should see 57 as the median.

Check this by sorting the data into descending order by score, then counting up to the 12th student, Kate. (She's the middle student and scored 57.)

(6) Enter 'Percentile' in cell A30, 0.75 in cell C30 and then make cell B30 active.

(7) Choose **Formulas>More Functions>Statistical>PERCENTILE.EXC.**

(8) Enter the range B4:B26 and C30 as the **K** value.

The reported value is 68, the figure which divides the top quarter from the bottom three-quarters of students.

(9) Enter 'Mode' in cell A31 then make cell B31 active.

(10) Choose **Formulas>More Functions>Statistical>Mode**.

(11) Enter the range B4:B26.

The reported value is 65 (that occurs more frequently than any other score).

5.4 Histograms

AAT only require knowledge of histograms, and what their uses are in business. Note that you will not be asked to reproduce these in the live assessment, however you need to understand what they are and how they work.

A **histogram** is a graph which shows the frequency with which certain values occur. Usually the values are grouped so that one could produce a histogram showing how many people were 160–165cm tall, how many >165–170, >170–175 and so on.

Excel can produce histogram analyses provided the **Analysis ToolPak** is installed. Installation was described earlier in the section about time series.

To demonstrate the histogram we will use the 'Student results' spreadsheet again.

Illustration 11: Histogram preparation

(1) Open the 'Student Results' spreadsheet if it is not already open.

You will see that in E5 to E13 is a column called 'Bins'. This describes the groupings that we want our results to be included in, so here we are going up the result in groups (bins) of ten percentage points at a time; the histogram will show how many results are in 0–10, 11–20, 21–30 etc.

(2) Choose **Data>Data Analysis>Histogram**.

(3) Enter the range B4:B26 as the **Input Range**.

(4) Enter E5:E13 as the **Bin Range**.

(5) Choose **New Worksheet Ply** and enter 'Histogram analysis' in the white text box.

(6) Tick **Chart Output**.

(7) Click on **OK**.

The new worksheet will show the data grouped into the 'bins' by frequency and also shows a histogram.

The spreadsheet 'Student Results Finished' shows the finished spreadsheet complete with histogram in the 'Histogram analysis' sheet.

---

6 Combination charts

Excel allows you to combine two different charts into one. For example, you may wish to compare sales to profits. This is also known as showing two graphs on one axis.

To do this we create a chart from our data as before.

Illustration 12: Combination charts

(1) Open the 'Combination chart' spreadsheet from the downloaded files. This provides data for the number of sales of precious metal in 2009 and 2010. The price at which the precious metal is sold per kilo goes up and down according to the market.

(2) Select the data that will go into your chart (cells A1 to C9)

(3) Click **Insert** and then choose your chart type. For this example let's choose a **2-D clustered column** chart. The chart doesn't really help us to understand the relationship between the two different sets of data.

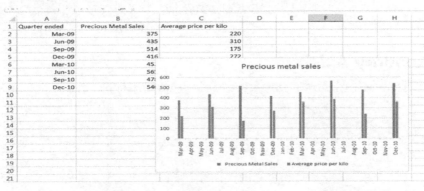

(4) A more visual way of displaying the average price data might be to see it in a line set against the number of sales. So click on any Average price column, right-click and select **Change Series Chart Type**.

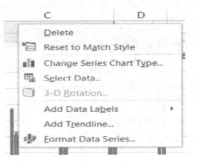

(5) Select **Line with Markers** and click **OK**. The chart will look like this:

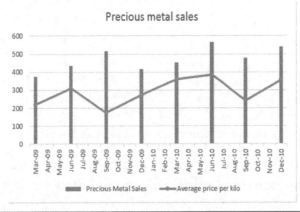

(6) The chart still does not make sense, as the figures on the left axis are not comparing like with like. So we need to right-click again an Average price marker and choose **Format Data Series**.

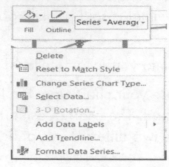

(7) Click **Secondary Axis**.

(8) Click **OK**.

(9) Take some time to play with the **Chart Tools**. Give the chart the name 'Precious metal sales' and label the axes. The vertical axis on the left should show the number of sales, while the right-hand axis should show the price per kilo.

You should end up with a chart that looks something like:

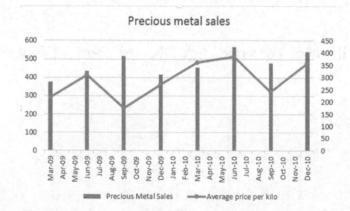

It can clearly be seen that the price per kilo dips in the third quarter of each year, something we could not easily determine without using the combination chart.

7 Error detection and correction

It is important to try to detect and correct errors before a spreadsheet is used to make decisions. We've already looked at some ways of trying to prevent wrong input (for example, data validation).

The final part of this chapter covers Excel's built-in help facility, error messages and ways to check that a spreadsheet has been constructed and is being used correctly.

7.1 Help

You can use Excel's Help window to quickly find the answer to any questions you may have while using Excel. You can access Help by clicking the **Help** button (question mark symbol) in the top-right corner of your spreadsheet or by pressing **F1**.

You can either type a search term directly into the white bar, or click on the **book icon** to access a table of help contents.

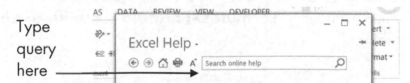

Take some time to explore the results when you type in different search terms. For example, if you found the section on **What If** analysis challenging, you could type 'What if' into the search bar to receive help on this topic.

7.2 Removing circular references

Although AAT no longer test this as part of the synoptic assessment, we cover this area here as there is often a time when the error will appear on more complex spreadsheets or where lots of formula are being used. Therefore, it is useful to know how to correct such problems.

Occasionally there is an issue with the formula whereby it has been set up incorrectly, linking it into an 'endless circle'. In the example below, the cell B5 is a total of the cells B3-B4. However, a formula has been entered in B4 which also refers to B5. This is called a **circular reference**.

Circular references nearly always mean that there's a mistake in the logic of the spreadsheet. Here's an example:

	A	B
1		
2		£
3	Basic salary	20,000
4	Bonus 10% of total pay	=0.1*B5
5	Total pay	20,000
6		

A warning will be displayed by Excel:

Microsoft Excel

⚠ Careful, we found one or more circular references in your workbook that might cause your formulas to calculate incorrectly.

FYI: A circular reference can be a formula that refers to its own cell value, or refers to a cell dependent on its own cell value.

[OK]   [Help]

In our example, it is relatively easy to find the cause of the problem, but in a large spreadsheet it can be difficult. Clicking **OK** will provide help and will bring up a help screen referring you to **Formulas>Formula Auditing>Circular References** on the Ribbon.

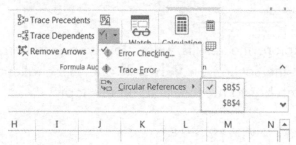

7.3 Using trace precedents

Tracing precedents and dependents

As spreadsheets are developed it can become difficult to be sure where figures come from and go to (despite being able to display formulas in all the cells). A useful technique is to make use of the 'trace precedents' and 'trace dependents' options. These are available on the **Formulas** section of the Ribbon.

Illustration 13: Auditing formulas

(1) Open the 'Precedent example' spreadsheet from the downloaded files and make cell F4 active.

(2) Choose the **Formulas** section of the Ribbon and click on **Trace Precedents** in the **Formula Auditing** group of icons.

You should see:

	A	B	C	D	E	F
1	BUDGETED SALES FIGURES					
2		Jan	Feb	Mar		Total
3		£'000	£'000	£'000		£'000
4	North	2,431	3,001	2,189		7,621
5	South	6,532	5,826	6,124		18,482
6	West	895	432	596		1,923
7	Total	9,858	9,259	8,909		28,026
8						
9						
10						
11						

Now it is very obvious that anything in column E, like April figures, will not be included in the total.

(3) Click on **Remove Arrows** in the **Formula Auditing** group.

(4) Make B4 the active cell.

(5) Click on **Trace Dependents**. This will show what cells make use of this cell:

	A	B	C	D	E	F
1	BUDGETED SALES FIGURES					
2		Jan	Feb	Mar		Total
3		£'000	£'000	£'000		£'000
4	North	2,431	3,001	2,189		7,621
5	South	6,532	5,826	6,124		18,482
6	West	895	432	596		1,923
7	Total	9,858	9,259	8,909		28,026
8						

Assessment focus point

Although AAT have stated that that you will be tested on the ability to trace precedents and dependents, it is a valuable skill in being able to check your spreadsheet for any potential problems, and useful in auditing formulas (which is a skill tested by the AAT).

7.4 Rounding errors

The ability to display numbers in a variety of formats (eg to no decimal places) can result in a situation whereby totals that are correct may actually look incorrect.

Illustration 14: Rounding errors

The following illustrations show how apparent rounding errors can arise.

	A	B	C
1	*Petty cash*		
2	Week ending 31/12/20X6		
3			£
4	Opening balance		231.34
5	Receipts		32.99
6	Payments		-104.67
7	Closing balance		159.66

	A	B	C
1	*Petty cash*		
2	Week ending 31/12/20X6		
3			£
4	Opening balance		231
5	Receipts		33
6	Payments		-105
7	Closing balance		160

Cell C7 contains the formula =SUM(C4:C6). The spreadsheet on the left shows the correct total to two decimal places. The spreadsheet on the right seems to be saying that 231 + 33 – 105 is equal to 160, which is not true: it's 159 (check it). The **reason for the discrepancy** is that both spreadsheets actually contain the values shown in the spreadsheet on the **left**.

However, the spreadsheet on the right has been formatted to display numbers with **no decimal places**. So, individual numbers display as the nearest whole number, although the actual value held by the spreadsheet and used in calculations includes the decimals.

The round function

One solution that will prevent the appearance of apparent errors is to use the **ROUND function**. The ROUND function has the following structure: ROUND (value, places). 'Value' is the value to be rounded. 'Places' is the number of places to which the value is to be rounded.

The difference between using the ROUND function and formatting a value to a number of decimal places is that using the ROUND function actually **changes** the **value**, while formatting only changes the **appearance** of the value.

In the example above, the ROUND function could be used as follows. The following formulas could be inserted in cells D4 to D7.

D4 = ROUND(C4,0)
D5 = ROUND(C5,0)
D6 = ROUND(C6,0)
D7 = Round (SUM(D4:D6),0)

Column C could then be hidden by highlighting the whole column (clicking on the C at the top of the column), then right-clicking anywhere on the column and selecting **Hide**. Try this for yourself, using the 'Rounding example' spreadsheet.

D4		▾	⋮	✕	✓	*fx*	=ROUND(C4,0)

	A	B	D	E	F
1	*Petty cash*				
2	Week ending 31/12/20X6				
3					
4	Opening balance		231		
5	Receipts		33.00		
6	Payments		-105.00		
7	Closing balance		159.00		

Note that using the ROUND function to eliminate decimals results in slightly inaccurate calculation totals (in our example 160 is actually 'more correct' than the 159 obtained using ROUND). For this reason, some people prefer not to use the function, and to make users of the spreadsheet aware that small apparent differences are due to rounding.

Roundup and Rounddown

The ROUND function can be adapted to round numbers to a required number of decimal places, either by rounding up, rounding down.

Roundup

For example, if a cost per unit was £100.828392 and management wished to express this value rounded up to 0, 1, and 2 decimal places then the following **Roundup** formulas could be used.

	A	B	C
1	**Costs**	**Rounding required**	**Roundup**
2	100.828392	0	=ROUNDUP(A2,B2)
3	100.828392	1	=ROUNDUP(A3,B3)
4	100.828392	2	=ROUNDUP(A4,B4)

Looking at the formula shown in cell C2 the A2 reference picks up the value to be rounded, and B2 is the number of decimal places to round up to. In C2 we are requesting Excel to round the value up to zero places, and so on.

The rounded up results would then be as follows.

	A	B	C
1	**Costs**	**Rounding required**	**Roundup**
2	£100.828392	0	£101.00
3	£100.828392	1	£100.90
4	£100.828392	2	£100.83

Using the same value £100.828392 and using the Rounddown formula, the formulas would be.

	A	B	C
1	Costs	Rounding required	Rounddown
2	100.828392	0	=ROUNDDOWN(A2,B2)
3	100.828392	1	=ROUNDDOWN(A3,B3)
4	100.828392	2	=ROUNDDOWN(A4,B4)

The rounded down results would be as follows.

	A	B	C
1	Costs	Rounding required	Rounddown
2	£100.828392	0	£100.00
3	£100.828392	1	£100.80
4	£100.828392	2	£100.82

7.5 Identifying error values

Error checking can be turned on by **File button>Excel options>Formulas** and checking **Enable background error checking**. There is a list that allows you to decide which errors to be highlighted. If a green triangle appears in a cell, then the cell contains an error.

#NUM!

Other information about the nature of the error will also be supplied:

#########	The column is not wide enough to hold the number. Widen the column or choose another format in which to display the number (no green triangle here, as it is not a 'real' error – just a presentation problem).
#DIV/0!	Commonly caused by a formula attempting to divide a number by zero (perhaps because the divisor cell is blank).
#VALUE!	Occurs when a mathematical formula refers to a cell containing text; eg if cell A2 contains text, then the formula =A1+A2+A3 will return #VALUE! Functions that operate on ranges (eg SUM) will not result in a #VALUE! error as they ignore text values.
#NAME?	The formula contains text that is not a valid cell address, range name or function name. Check the spelling of any functions used (eg by looking through functions under **Formulas>Insert Function**).

#REF!	The formula includes an invalid cell reference, for example a reference to cells that have subsequently been deleted.
	If you notice the reference immediately after a deletion, use **Ctrl+Z** to reverse the deletion.
#NUM!	This error is caused by invalid numeric values being supplied to a worksheet formula or function. For example, using a negative number with the **SQRT** (square root) function.
	To investigate, check the formula and function logic and syntax. The **Formula Auditing** toolbar may help this process (see below).
#N/A	A value is not available to a function or formula; for example omitting a required argument from a spreadsheet function. Again, the **Formula Auditing** toolbar may help the investigation process (see below).

7.6 Tracing and correcting errors

If you do see one of the above errors you can trace where it came from by clicking on the cell with the error, then, from the **Formulas** tab of the Ribbon, choose **Formula Auditing** and click the down arrow next to **Error Checking**. Lines will appear pointing to the data that has produced the error.

If you simply click the **Error Checking** button, it will automatically check the current worksheet and alert you to any errors.

Finally, you can click **Evaluate Formula** to be taken step-by-step through it so that you can identify the error.

8 Reporting accounting information

You will be able to use a variety of tools and have developed your skills in using spreadsheets to analyse and present data. In the exam it is vital that you answer the question, following closely any instructions regarding presentation and data to be analysed. Sometimes the question may specify the type of presentation (table, graph, chart) and sometimes the examiner will ask you to use your own judgement on how to best present the information.

You may be tested on your ability to be able to differentiate between what information is required and what will not aid you answering the question.

Practice using the spreadsheet tools using the illustrations, examples and test your learning questions provided. Ensure that you can organise, analyse and present the data in the most efficient and appropriate manner.

The ten **practice activities** at the end of this book will give valuable practice in making judgements on how to apply functions and formulas in specific situations to obtain the required output.

Chapter summary

- It is important to save and **backup your work regularly**. You can use **Save as** to give various versions of the same document different names.

- It is important to **control the security** of spreadsheets through passwords, locking (protecting) cells against unauthorised or accidental changes, or data validation on input.

- Spreadsheet packages permit the user to work with **multiple sheets** that refer to each other. This is sometimes referred to as a three-dimensional spreadsheet.

- Excel offers sophisticated data handling, including **filtering**, **pivot tables** and **look-up tables**.

- **Combination charts** allow you to show two sets of data on one axis of your chart.

- **Goal seek** is a function that allows you to explore various results using different sets of values in one or more formulas.

- **Error detection** and prevention is important in spreadsheet design and testing. There are useful facilities available, such as tracing precedents and dependents, identification of circular references, and error reports, as well as Excel's built-in help function.

- It is important to make judgements on how to apply functions and formulas when using spreadsheet software when **reporting accounting information**.

Keywords

- **Backup:** Where a copy file is taken so work can be restored if original work is lost or destroyed

- **Cell locking:** A data protection method that prevents users from changing the content of locked cells

- **Circular references:** Situations where a cell contains a formula and the same cell reference is itself in the formula cell

- **Data table:** A table that allows data results to change, based on changing assumptions

- **Data validation:** A function that can provide warning messages and other protection when invalid data is entered

- **Find and replace:** Method of locating specific data in a worksheet and replacing with alternative data if required

- **Formula auditing:** An error-checking approach that shows the connections between formulas and cells

- **Goal seek:** Function that can identify the inputs required into a formula to arrive at a known outcome

- **Histogram:** A graph which shows the frequency with which certain values occur

- **Look-up tables:** A function that allows users to find and use data held in a table

- **Mean:** An average value calculated by adding up values and dividing by the number of values

- **Median:** The value that is the middle value when values are arranged in an ascending or descending sequence

- **Mode:** The most frequently occurring value within a sequence of values

- **Moving average:** A technique that evens out any seasonal variations so that trends can be more easily identified

- **Passwords:** A data protection system that restricts user access by a unique sequence of characters

- **Pivot table:** A table that allows users to change its structure by selecting and choosing the style of how data is presented

- **Save:** The process of 'saving' the contents of a file so that any work completed is retained. The action of saving will overwrite the existing file

- **Save as:** Similar to save, but the file being 'saved as' is given a different name

- **Scenarios:** A function that allows users to change information to discover how changes can alter the outcome of a scenario

- **Sort and filter:** A function that allows data to be sorted in a requested order, for example A-Z. A filter allows users to select and display part of the contents of a table of data

- **Trace precedents and dependents:** Error-detection methods that use tracer arrows to identify data used in formulas and relationships between active cells

Test your learning

1 **What command is used to save a file under a different name?**

2 **What part of the Ribbon do you go to set up checking procedures on the input of data?**

3 **List three possible uses for a multi-sheet (3D) spreadsheet.**

4 **What does filtering do?**

5 **What is a trend line?**

6 **What is the median?**

7 **What is a histogram?**

8 **What does the error message #DIV/0! mean?**

Test your learning: answers

Chapter 1 Introduction to spreadsheets (Excel 2010)

1   Text, values or formulae.

2   F5 opens a GoTo dialogue box which is useful for navigating around large spreadsheets. F2 puts the active cell into edit mode.

3   You can use the technique of 'filling' – selecting the first few items of a series and dragging the lower-right corner of the selection in the appropriate direction.

4   Select **Formulas** on the Ribbon then click **Show Formulas**. Alternatively press **Ctrl + `**.

5   Removing gridlines, adding shading, adding borders, using different fonts and font sizes, presenting numbers as percentages or currency or to a certain number of decimal places.

6   =IF(logical test, value if true, value if false)

7   (a)   =Sum(B4:B5) or =B4+B5
    (b)   =Sum(B5:D5)
    (c)   =Sum(E4:E5) or =Sum(B6:D6) or best of all, to check for errors:
          =IF(SUM(E4:E5)= Sum(B6:D6), Sum(B6:D6),"Error")

8   (a)   =SUM(B4:B8)
    (b)   =C9*D1
    (c)   =D9+D10 or =D9*(1+D1)

Chapter 2 More advanced spreadsheet techniques (Excel 2010)

1   **Save as**

2   **Data > Data Validation**

3   The construction of a spreadsheet model with separate Input, Calculation and Output sheets. They can help consolidate data from different sources. They can offer different views of the same data.

4   Filtering allows you to see only areas of a table where there are certain values. Other items are filtered from view.

5   The trend line shows how one variable (for example, cost) changes as another does (for example, volume of production).

6   If data is ranked in ascending or descending order, the median is the value of the middle item.

7   A graph which shows the frequency with which certain values occur.

8   An error commonly caused by dividing a number by zero.

Chapter 3 Introduction to spreadsheets (Excel 2013)

1   Text, values or formulae.

2   F5 opens a GoTo dialogue box which is useful for navigating around large spreadsheets. F2 puts the active cell into edit mode.

3   You can use the technique of 'filling' – selecting the first few items of a series and dragging the lower-right corner of the selection in the appropriate direction.

4   Select **Formulas** on the Ribbon then click **Show Formulas**. Alternatively press **Ctrl** + `.

5   Removing gridlines, adding shading, adding borders, using different fonts and font sizes, presenting numbers as percentages or currency or to a certain number of decimal places.

6   =IF(logical test, value if true, value if false)

7   (a)   =Sum(B4:B5) or =B4+B5
     (b)   =Sum(B5:D5)
     (c)   =Sum(E4:E5) or =Sum(B6:D6) or, best of all, to check for errors: =IF(SUM(E4:E5)= Sum(B6:D6), Sum(B6:D6),"Error")

8   (a)   =SUM(B4:B8)
     (b)   =C9*D1
     (c)   =D9+D10 or =D9*(1+D1)

Chapter 4 More advanced spreadsheet techniques (Excel 2013)

1   **Save as**

2   **Data > Data Validation**

3   The construction of a spreadsheet model with separate Input, Calculation and Output sheets. They can help consolidate data from different sources. They can offer different views of the same data.

4   Filtering allows you to see only areas of a table where there are certain values. Other items are filtered from view.

5   The trend line shows how one variable (for example, cost) changes as another does (for example, volume of production).

6   If data is ranked in ascending or descending order the median is the value of the middle item.

7   A graph which shows the frequency with which certain values occur.

8   An error commonly caused by dividing a number by zero.

Practice activities

These activities enable you to practise some of the skills and techniques introduced in earlier chapters.

The activities are suitable for both Excel 2010 and Excel 2013.

Each activity requires you to create or open a specified spreadsheet with a matching name and suffix eg 'Activity 1'.

No printed answers are provided, but a spreadsheet which solves the activity will have a matching name with suffix 'Answer', eg 'Activity 1 Answer'.

The opening spreadsheets and answers for each activity are provided in the files available for download from https://learningmedia.bpp.com/catalog?pagename =AAT_Spreadsheets

Some activities have no initial spreadsheet. The answer is a spreadsheet with the appropriate activity reference.

Activity		Subject
1	Zumbo	Formatting
2	IML	Charts
3	Cash flow exercise	General spreadsheet design
4	Dittori	General spreadsheet design
5	Pivot	Pivot table
6	Height and weight	Data manipulation and statistical functions
7	Retirement	Lookup and IF functions
8	Check data	Data validation
9	Order form	Lookup
10	Employees	Functions

Activity 1: Zumbo

Open the spreadsheet 'Activity 1 Question'.

	A	B	C	D	E
1	Zumbo Enterprises Ltd				
2					
3	Invoice				
4					
5	Date		40608		
6	Account		2141432		
7	Customer		J Jones		
8			21 The Cutting, Anytown AY1 2WR		
9					
10	Product cc	Product description	Quantity	Unit price	Net
11					£
12	1234	2 metre steel bar	10	12.33	123.3
13					0
14					0
15					0
16					0
17	Total net				123.3
18	VAT	0.20			24.66
19	Total Gross				147.96

Required

Format the layout so that the screen looks more like:

	A	B	C	D	E
1	**Zumbo Enterprises Ltd**				
2					
3	**Invoice**				
4					
5	Date		06 March 2011		
6	Account		2141432		
7	Customer		J Jones		
8			21 The Cutting, Anytown AY1 2WR		
9					
10	**Product code**	**Product description**	**Quantity**	**Unit price**	**Net**
11					£
12	1234	2 metre steel bar	10	12.33	123.30
13					0.00
14					0.00
15					0.00
16					0.00
17	Total net				123.30
18	VAT		20%		24.66
19	**Total Gross**				147.96
20					

Adjust font, borders, alignment, cell colour and number of decimal places to improve presentation.

Activity 2: IML

Open the spreadsheet 'Activity 2 Question'.

	A	B	C	D	E
1	International Magazines Limited: Sales by Region Jan-Jun 2011				
2		Europe	America	Rest of the world	Total
3	Woman's Day	251,208	163,514	105,000	£ 519,722
4	Blue!	202,262	136,290	78,485	£ 417,036
5	Easy Cooking	143,588	86,040	114,900	£ 344,528
6	Sorted!	27,796	6,234	14,769	£ 48,798
7	Total	£624,852	£392,078	£313,154	£1,330,083

You work in the accounts department of International Magazines Limited (IML). IML publishes four magazines, which are sold throughout the world. One of the spreadsheets you work on, shown above, analyses sales by magazine and world region.

Required

Follow the instructions below to create several charts using the Chart Wizard.

(a)   **Select cells A2:D6 (ensure these are the only cells selected, do not include the totals).**

(b)   **Use the chart wizard button to insert three charts of that data: 2D clustered column, 2D stacked column and 3D clustered column.**

(c)   **Enter a suitable title for each graph.**

(d)   **Adjust their sizes and positions by obtaining the correct pointer shape, holding down the mouse button and dragging.**

**Changes
chart
position**

**Changes
chart
shape**

Activity 3: Cash flow exercise

You want to set up a simple six-month cash flow projection in such a way that you can use it to estimate how the **projected cash balance** figures will **change** in total when any **individual item** in the projection is **altered**. You have the following information.

(a) Sales were £45,000 per month in 20X5, falling to £42,000 in January 20X6. Thereafter they are expected to increase by 3% per month (ie February will be 3% higher than January, and so on).

(b) Debts are collected as follows.

    (i)   60% in month following sale

    (ii)   30% in second month after sale

    (iii) 7% in third month after sale

    (iv) 3% remains uncollected

(c) Purchases are equal to cost of sales, set at 65% of sales.

(d) Overheads were £6,000 per month in 20X5, rising by 5% in 20X6.

(e) Opening cash is an overdraft of £7,500.

(f) Dividends: £10,000 final dividend on 20X5 profits, payable in May.

(g) Capital purchases: plant costing £18,000 will be ordered in January. 20% is payable with order, 70% on delivery in February and the final 10% in May.

Setting up the assumptions area

These assumptions have been set up in an opening spreadsheet for you.

Open the file 'Activity 3 – Assumptions'. Columns B and G contain the numbers or values making up the assumptions to be used in the cash flow exercise.

	D13			f_x	Payable May					
	A	B	C	D	E	F	G	H	
4									
5	Historical monthly sales 2005 (£)	45,000		Purchases = cost of sales.			65%	of sales	
6	Projected sales Jan 20X6 (£)	42,000		Monthly overheads 20X5 (£)			6,000		
7	Monthly sales growth (20X6 onwards)	3%		Rise in monthly overheads 20X6			5%		
8	Collection of debts:			Opening cash balance (O/d)			-7,500		
9	Month following sales	60%		Dividends (payable May 20X6, £)			10,000		
10	2nd month following sales	30%		Capital expenditure			18,000		
11	3rd month following sales	7%		Payable January			20%		
12	Uncollected	3%		Payable February			70%		
13				Payable May			10%		
14									
15									

Required

Design a spreadsheet to give a cash flow forecast for six months (January to June).

Activity 4: Dittori

Dittori Ltd has a sales ledger package which does not offer an aged receivables option. You have decided to set up a simple spreadsheet to monitor ageing by region. You have been able to export the following information from the sales ledger, as at 31 May 20X6. This data is contained in a spreadsheet – file 'Activity 4 Question'.

Region	Current	1 month	2 month	3 month	4 month	5 month +
Highlands	346.60	567.84	32.17	–	–	54.8
Strathclyde	24,512.05	28,235.50	4,592.50	1,244.80	51.36	942.57
Borders	1,927.77	–	512.88	–	–	–
North West	824.80	14,388.91	2,473.53	–	482.20	79.66
North East	14,377.20	12,850.00	–	3,771.84	1,244.55	–
Midlands	45,388.27	61,337.88	24,001.02	4,288.31	1,391.27	4,331.11
Wales	14,318.91	5,473.53	21.99	4,881.64	512.27	422.5
East Anglia	157.20	943.68	377.40	1,500.87	15.33	247.66
South West	9,528.73	11,983.39	3,771.89	6,228.77	1,008.21	214.51
South East	60,110.70	83,914.54	29,117.96	24,205.10	14,320.90	5,422.50
France	6,422.80	7,451.47	5,897.55	2,103.70	140.50	3,228.76
Other EU	5,433.88	4,991.90	5,012.70	4,223.80	1,022.43	1,984.29
Rest of World	1,822.70	4,529.67	277.50	3,491.34	–	–

Required

Prepare a spreadsheet which will extend the above analysis to total receivables by region and the percentage of debt in each age category and the percentage by region.

Activity 5: Pivot

Open the file 'Activity 5 Question'. An extract from this spreadsheet is shown below.

	A	B	C	D
1	Issue No	Quantity	Colour	Shape
2	1473	159	Blue	Square
3	1474	84	Yellow	Square
4	1475	120	Green	Triangular
5	1476	125	Blue	Round
6	1477	153	Yellow	Triangular
7	1478	99	Blue	Round
8	1479	137	Blue	Triangular
9	1480	199	Red	Square
10	1481	16	Red	Round
11	1482	158	Green	Square
12	1483	29	Red	Triangular
13	1484	118	Yellow	Square
14	1485	167	Blue	Round
15	1486	177	Red	Triangular
16	1487	168	Green	Square
17	1488	110	Red	Round
18	1489	181	Red	Square
19	1490	168	Blue	Square
20	1491	31	Red	Square
21	1492	86	Green	Triangular
22	1493	160	Green	Triangular
23	1494	120	Red	Square
24	1495	101	Blue	Triangular
25	1496	141	Red	Triangular
26	1497	187	Blue	Triangular
27	1498	62	Green	Square
28	1499	177	Blue	Triangular
29	1500	148	Green	Square
30	1501	175	Red	Triangular
31	1502	131	Red	Square
32	1503	67	Blue	Square
33	1504	18	Blue	Round

The spreadsheet shows the quantity of components of various types that were issued from stores to production during a period. Components come in four colours (blue, red, green and yellow) and three shapes (square, round and triangular).

Required

Use Microsoft Excel's Pivot Table feature to analyse and summarise this data by colour and by shape in a two-dimensional table, as shown below:

Sum of quantity	Colour				
Shape	Blue	Green	Red	Yellow	Grand total
Round					
Square					
Triangular					
Grand total					

Activity 6: Height and weight

The spreadsheet 'Activity 6 Question' contains data about a number of people's height and weight. Open that spreadsheet. The data is presently in alphabetical order by name of person.

Required

Just below the list of data use statistical functions to work out:

(a) **Mean height and mean weight (175.56, 70.3)**

(b) **Number of people in the sample (25)**

(c) **Minimum height and minimum weight (169, 58.2)**

(d) **Maximum height and maximum weight (182, 84.5)**

(e) **Mode for height and mode for weight (the most common readings, 175, 67.4)**

(f) **Median for height and median for weight (the middle reading, 175, 70.1)**

(g) **Sort the table of data by height and check the mode and median obtained for height**

(h) **Sort the table of data by weight and check the mode and median obtained for weight**

(i) **Draw a scatter graph of weight (y) against height (x)**

(j) **Use the Trend function to estimate, to one decimal place, the weight of someone who is 175.5 cm tall (70.2 kg)**

(k) **Set up a bin range on your spreadsheet with values of 169, 170, ...182, and produce a histogram for heights**

Activity 7: Retirement

Open the spreadsheet 'Activity 7 Question'.

	A	B
1	Retirement age	65
2		
3	Name	Vic
4	Age	66
5		
6	Years to retirement	Retired
7		
8		
9	Name	Age
10	Annette	38
11	Josephine	43
12	Mike	32
13	Paula	70
14	Vandana	42
15	Omar	34
16	Vic	66
17		

Required

(a) **In B4 insert a VLOOKUP function which will display the age of the person whose name is typed into cell B3.**

(b) **In B6 insert the number of years to retirement (with reference to the value in B1). If the person has reached retirement age or is older B6 should state 'Retired'.**

Activity 8: Check data

Open the spreadsheet 'Activity 8 Question'.

Required

(a) **Change the font to Arial, size 10, apart from the title 'Questionnaire Analysis'. Change the headings to Arial size 12, bold and red. Adjust column widths if necessary.**

(b) **Sort the table into female and male.**

(c) **You need to use data validation to ensure that only people aged between 30 and 50 are to be included.**

(d) **Show all cells which are outside of the data validation, take a screenshot (Alt + Print Screen) and paste it into a new worksheet named 'Validation'.**

Activity 9: Order form

You will use a LOOKUP function to determine the rate of discount to be used when buying items from a wholesale retailer.

Open the workbook 'Activity 9 Question'.

Required

(a)   **Enter 12 in cell B7.**

(b)   **Enter a HLOOKUP function in cell B9 to return the correct discount rate for the number of items ordered. Format this cell as percentage.**

(c)   **Enter a formula in cell B11 to calculate the value of the order before discount.**

(d)   **Enter a formula in cell E11 to calculate the discount based on the rate shown in cell B9.**

(e)   **Enter a formula in cell B13 to calculate the value of the order after discount.**

(f)   **Now enter a VLOOKUP function in cell B9 to return the correct discount rate for the items ordered.**

You should get the same answers as when using the HLOOKUP function.

Activity 10: Employees

Open the workbook 'Activity 10 Question'.

Required

(a)   **Insert a column between Date of birth and Department and title it as Age.**

Using 31 March 2016 as the current date, calculate the age of each employee.

(b)   **It has been decided to give a £25 bonus to all employees over the age of 40 (ie employees aged 40 and above) who have had fewer than 2 days' absence in the year.**

Enter Bonus in cell G1.

Use a nested IF function in cell G2, entering 25 in the Value_if_true field and 0 in the Value_if_false field (ie If age is greater than or equal to 40 *and* absence is less than 2, then a bonus is due).

Copy this formula down the Bonus column.

(c)   **In cell C22 enter Number of employees over 40. Use the COUNTIF function in cell D22 to calculate the number of employees over 40.**

In cell C23 enter Average age of employees. Use the AVERAGE function in cell D23 to calculate the average age of employees.

(d) Label cell H1 Retirement year.

In cell H2 use the YEAR function to find the year of birth for each employee and add 66 to it – this will give the year in which the employee can retire.

Copy this formula down the Retirement year column.

(e) Insert a column between First and Date of birth and title it as Name.

Use the CONCATENATE function to join together the First name and Surname with a space in between. Hide columns A and B. Hide zeros in columns Absence and Bonus.

Glossary of terms

It is useful to be familiar with interchangeable terminology including IFRS and UK GAAP (generally accepted accounting principles).

Below is a short list of the most important terms you are likely to use or come across, together with their international and UK equivalents.

UK term	International term
Profit and loss account	**Statement of profit or loss (or statement of profit or loss and other comprehensive income)**
Turnover or Sales	Revenue or Sales revenue
Operating profit	Profit from operations
Reducing balance depreciation	Diminishing balance depreciation
Depreciation / depreciation expense(s)	Depreciation charge(s)
Balance sheet	**Statement of financial position**
Fixed assets	Non-current assets
Net book value	Carrying amount
Tangible assets	Property, plant and equipment
Stocks	Inventories
Trade debtors or Debtors	Trade receivables
Prepayments	Other receivables
Debtors and prepayments	Trade and other receivables
Cash at bank and in hand	Cash and cash equivalents
Long-term liabilities	Non-current liabilities
Trade creditors or creditors	Trade payables
Accruals	Other payables
Creditors and accruals	Trade and other payables
Capital and reserves	Equity (limited companies)
Profit and loss balance	Retained earnings
Cash flow statement	**Statement of cash flows**

Accountants often have a tendency to use several phrases to describe the same thing! Some of these are listed below:

Different terms for the same thing
Nominal ledger, main ledger or general ledger
Subsidiary ledgers, memorandum ledgers
Subsidiary (sales) ledger, sales ledger
Subsidiary (purchases) ledger, purchases ledger

Index

Notes

REVIEW FORM

How have you used this Course Book?
(Tick one box only)

☐ Self study

☐ On a course_____

☐ Other _____

Why did you decide to purchase this Course Book? *(Tick one box only)*

☐ Have used BPP materials in the past

☐ Recommendation by friend/colleague

☐ Recommendation by a college lecturer

☐ Saw advertising

☐ Other _____

During the past six months do you recall seeing/receiving either of the following?
(Tick as many boxes as are relevant)

☐ Our advertisement in Accounting Technician

☐ Our Publishing Catalogue

Which (if any) aspects of our advertising do you think are useful?
(Tick as many boxes as are relevant)

☐ Prices and publication dates of new editions

☐ Information on Course Book content

☐ Details of our free online offering

☐ None of the above

Your ratings, comments and suggestions would be appreciated on the following areas of this Course Book.

	Very useful	Useful	Not useful
Chapter overviews	☐	☐	☐
Introductory section	☐	☐	☐
Quality of explanations	☐	☐	☐
Illustrations	☐	☐	☐
Chapter activities	☐	☐	☐
Test your learning	☐	☐	☐
Keywords	☐	☐	☐

	Excellent	Good	Adequate	Poor
Overall opinion of this Course Book	☐	☐	☐	☐

Do you intend to continue using BPP Products? ☐ Yes ☐ No

Please note any further comments and suggestions/errors on the reverse of this page. The BPP author of this edition can be emailed at: lmfeedback@bpp.com

Alternatively, the Head of Programme of this edition can be emailed at: nisarahmed@bpp.com

REVIEW FORM (continued)

TELL US WHAT YOU THINK

Please note any further comments and suggestions/errors below